THE
CANADIAN
SHORT
STORY

DATE DUE

Perspectives on Canadian Culture

JUDITH SALTMAN
Modern Canadian Children's Books

EUGENE BENSON & L.W. CONOLLY
English-Canadian Theatre

DAVID CLANDFIELD
Canadian Film

MICHELLE GADPAILLE
The Canadian Short Story

EDITH FOWKE
Canadian Folklore

Forthcoming:

PENNY PETRONE
Canadian Indian Literature

MERVIN BUTOVSKY
Canadian Jewish Writers

DAVID KETTERER
Canadian Science Fiction and Fantasy

ALICE VAN WART
Canadian Diaries and Journals

DONNA BENNETT
Canadian Literary Criticism

DOUG FETHERLING
The Press in Canada

DAVID MATTISON
Canadian Photography

THE
CANADIAN
SHORT
STORY

Michelle Gadpaille

Toronto   OXFORD UNIVERSITY PRESS   1988

Oxford University Press, 70 Wynford Drive, Don Mills, Ontario, M3C 1J9

Toronto Oxford New York Delhi Bombay Calcutta Madras Karachi
Petaling Jaya Singapore Hong Kong Tokyo Nairobi Dar es Salaam
Cape Town Melbourne Auckland

and associated companies in
Berlin Ibadan

Canadian Cataloguing in Publication Data

Gadpaille, Michelle, 1953–
The Canadian short story

(Perspectives on Canadian culture)
Bibliography: p.
Includes index.
ISBN 0-19-540653-2

1. short stories, Canadian (English) – History and
criticism.* I. Title. II. Series.

PS8191.S5G32 1988   C813'.01'09   C88-094600-8
PR9192.52.G32 1988

CONTENTS

PREFACE

When it was suggested that I write a survey of the Canadian short story for the Perspectives on Canadian Culture series, I didn't at first see how it would be possible to cover over one hundred years of short fiction in a small book, while doing justice both to individual authors and to the historical overview. The finished book represents a compromise, containing three summary chapters—the first two and the last—treating historical periods and the past twenty-five years, and three chapters giving extended attention to the work of Canada's contemporary masters of the short story: Mavis Gallant, Alice Munro, and Margaret Atwood.

That these writers are all women is at once a fact and a literary enigma for anyone interested in studying this exceptionally strong genre of Canadian literature. Gallant, Munro, and Atwood, not to mention Audrey Thomas, must be read—but which of the many fine male writers since the 1960s also provide essential reading? The final chapter includes a personal selection, identifying particular stories by such diverse writers as Clark Blaise, Jack Hodgins, Hugh Hood, Alistair MacLeod, John Metcalf, W.D. Valgardson, and Guy Vanderhaeghe, among others—stories that certainly stand up to work of the women writers. It is difficult, however, to find collections by male writers that offer both reading satisfaction and complete representations of their writing at its best, such as one finds, for example, in *The Other Paris* (Gallant), *Something I've Been Meaning to Tell You* (Munro), *Dancing Girls* (Atwood), and *Goodbye Harold, Good Luck* (Thomas).

The dominance of women writers certainly reflects the story's recent tendency to turn inward, towards the body, the emotions, and ultimately the mind—territories that have not received sustained or primary attention by male writers in Canada. At the same time the short story has changed in the last twenty-five years. What is prized now is a brand of subtle subversion that goes beyond the post-modernist desire to fill the void left after the (largely male) American post-modernists deconstructed the well-made story. One aim of this 'new' story (written by Americans such as Bobbie Ann Mason and Alice Walker, as well as by Canadians Alice Munro, Margaret Atwood, and Audrey Thomas) is to affirm story-making as a force for exploration, understanding, and healing, and to create a literature out of everyday life that compels immediate recognition and identification. This appeal, which is both popular and literary, is a double base from which many of our women writers have been able to consolidate their hold on the public im-agination.

The brevity of a survey inevitably leads to the neglect of many accomplished writers. Among these are W.O. Mitchell, P.K. Page, Gwendolyn MacEwen, and Robert Kroetsch, whose main en-deavour and renown rest elsewhere. Stories by authors whose work lies outside the main traditions being outlined have also not been discussed: the charming romantic tales of Nova Scotia that Thomas Raddall published in the 1940s; the dense mythical parables of Sheila Watson; the lyrical stories of Elizabeth Spencer (who, after a long residence in Canada, has returned to the United States). And space alone has necessitated omitting from the final chapter an ap-preciation of the work of Edna Alford, Barry Callaghan, David Car-penter, Dave Godfrey, David Helwig, Joy Kogawa, Ken Mitchell, Bharati Mukherjee, Carol Shields, David Lewis Stein, Kent Thompson, Jane Urquhart, and Michael Yates. That so many writers clamour for attention is a testament to the vitality of the con-temporary short story in Canada.

I wish to thank William Toye and Patricia Sillers of Oxford Univer-sity Press Canada, who gave generously of their experience and time in the preparation of this book. I also wish to acknowledge the help and advice of Victor Kennedy, without whose computer expertise the manuscript would surely have gone astray between disk and database.

1

THE NINETEENTH CENTURY AND AFTER

The earliest antecedents of the Canadian short story rest in the writings of Thomas McCulloch and Thomas Chandler Haliburton, two Nova Scotians who were born in the eighteenth century, twenty years apart. They achieved contemporary popularity—and, in the case of Haliburton, international fame—not with stories as such but with humorous sketches containing narrative, dialogue, and sustaining characters that imaginatively and entertainingly advanced their own particular convictions. **Thomas McCulloch** (1776-1843), a Presbyterian minister who in 1838 became the first president of Dalhousie University, published in the *Acadian Recorder* (December 1821 to May 1822 and January-March 1823) his 'letters' of Mephibosheth Stepsure, which—in a succession of fictional incidents involving such comic figures (characterized by their names) as Parson Drone, the Reverend Shadrach Howl, Mr Soakem, and Mr Tipple—illustrate what he saw as a threat to moral values. Issued in book form in Halifax in 1860, *The Stepsure Letters* appeared exactly a century later in the New Canadian Library, with an introduction by Northrop Frye. **Thomas Chandler Haliburton** (1796-1865) was a practising lawyer, a member of the provincial assembly (1826-9), and of the Supreme Court of Nova Scotia (1841-56). In 1835-6 he contributed to the *Novascotian* a series of sketches that were published in 1836 as *The Clockmaker; or The Sayings and Doings of Samuel Slick, of Slickville* (New Canadian Library, 1958); other Sam Slick books followed. The narrator (Haliburton)—who travels about the province with Sam Slick, a clock salesman from Connecticut—relates the chance encounters, conversations laced with colourful frontier dialect and idiom, and ridiculous incidents that satirically oppose his own thrifty, shrewd, and industrious principles against the lackadaisical and extravagant habits of the British colonists and their offspring who seemed to be leading the province to ruin.

> 'What a pity it is, Mr Slick'—for such was his name—'what a pity it is,' said I, 'that you, who are so successful in teaching these people the value of clocks, could not also teach them the value of time.'

Slick admits that they are 'a most idle set of folks'.

> 'But how is it,' said I, 'that you manage to sell such an immense number of clocks, which certainly cannot be called necessary articles, among a people with whom there seems to be so great a scarcity of money?' Mr Slick paused, as if considering the propriety of answering the question, and looking me in the face, said in a confidential tone—
> 'Why, I don't care if I do tell you, for the market is glutted, and I shall quit this circuit. It is done by a knowledge of *soft sawder* and *human natur*'. But here is Deacon Flint's,' said he; 'I have but one clock left, and I guess I will sell it to him.'

Leaving the clock—much coveted, Slick claimed, by neighbour Steele's wife—with the Flints until he would return on his way back to the States, he relied on 'human natur' to effect the sale. 'We can do without any article or luxury we have never had, but when once obtained, it is not in "human natur" to surrender it voluntarily.'

The Sam Slick sketches have perhaps more significance as being among the first literary expressions of Canadian humour and irony than as early examples of the short story. Nevertheless they are a compact amalgam of incident, characterization, and narrative—and in Canadian literary history they belong to a tradition that three-quarters of a century later welcomed its greatest practitioner, **Stephen Leacock** (1869-1944).

In 1910 Leacock, who taught in the Department of Economics and Political Science at McGill University, published *Literary Lapses*, the first of many collections of his sketches, light essays, burlesques, and parodies that had previously appeared in periodicals and have made a signal contribution to comic literature. *Literary*

Lapses opens with 'My Financial Career'. Beginning with the famous words 'When I go into a bank I get rattled' and ending 'Since then I bank no more. I keep my money in cash in my trousers pocket and my savings in silver dollars in a sock', this sketch has attained the status of a classic miniature short story (it is little more than four pages long). It has often been anthologized as such, as have several chapters from Leacock's most popular books, *Sunshine Sketches of a Little Town* (1912) and *Arcadian Adventures of the Idle Rich* (1914), in which the 'sketches' are sustained narratives, more elaborate than usual, and are linked to form an artistic unity. 'The Marine Excursion of the Knights of Pythias' (*Sunshine Sketches*) describes a hilarious outing, with disastrous consequences, taken on Lake Wissanotti by the Knights of Pythias of the Ontario town of Mariposa (Orillia). 'The Rival Churches of St Asaph and St Osoph' (*Arcadian Adventures*) contrasts the characteristics of the Episcopalian (Anglican) clergyman of St Asaph's, which has 'brass tablets let into its walls, blackbirds singing in its elm trees, parishioners who dine at eight o'clock, and a rector who wears a little crucifix and dances the tango', with the gloomy and scholarly Presbyterian minister of St Osoph's, 'who was also honorary professor of philosophy at the university' and had spent 'fifty years in trying to reconcile Hegel with St Paul'. Both chapters transcend the genre of the sketch and have taken on a life of their own as 'stories'. These books are available in the New Canadian Library.

In the late nineteenth century, when Canadian writers of short fiction were no longer influenced by the eighteenth-century British models of the sketch and the extended satirical or humorous anecdote, they turned to a form that had become more particularly American than any other: the short story. Popularized by the earlier success of Edgar Allan Poe (*Tales of the Grotesque and Arabesque*, 1840) and Nathaniel Hawthorne (*Twice-Told Tales*, 1837; *Mosses from an Old Manse*, 1846), the short story entrenched itself in such popular magazines of the day as *Scribner's*, *Harper's*, and the *Atlantic Monthly,* among others. American magazines offered a market for Canadian writers, who seemed uninfluenced by the tradition of Poe (the detective and supernatural tale), of Hawthorne (New-World romance), or of O. Henry (the tightly plotted story with a surprise ending). In the late nineteenth century and after, the significant focus of Canadian short fiction lay in two other directions: the naturalistic animal story and the local-colour story. Charles G.D. Roberts and Ernest Thompson Seton invented the former genre; the story based on regional setting and character, however, was a continent-wide phenomenon.

At first glance the Canadian animal story—which gained immediate popularity—appears to be something of a dead-end in the march of fiction towards modernism. Conversely, the local-colour story, of more modest early sales, is usually accorded a privileged place in the development of the Canadian short story; ideals of realism, regionalism, and conservative narrative strategy remained dominant well past the middle of the twentieth century. Many of Roberts' and Seton's animal stories, however, have had a steady readership to this day—unlike the stories of the local-colour writers Gilbert Parker, E.W. Thomson, and the more polished stylists Duncan Campbell Scott and Sara Jeanette Duncan, interesting though some of them still are.

Sir Charles G.D. Roberts (1860-1943) had a long career as a man of letters—as poet, short-story writer, novelist, and the author of many works of non-fiction. With the poems he published between 1880 (the influential *Orion and Other Poems*) and 1893 (*Songs of the Common Day*), he became one of the leading Canadian poets of the late nineteenth century. His first animal story, 'Do Seek Their Meat from God', appeared in *Harper's* in December 1892 and was included with three others in *Earth's Enigmas: A Book of Animal and Nature Life* (1896). Its popularity led to *The Kindred of the Wild* (1902), *The Watchers of the Trails* (1904), *The Haunters of the Silences* (1907), and other less successful collections until 1936 (*Further Animal Stories*).

Roberts drew inspiration for his animal stories from his youthful wanderings in the New Brunswick countryside, particularly the Tantramar Marshes, and from his reading. To the knowledge of animal behaviour thus acquired, he added his exceptional gifts as a storyteller, and his poet's sensibility, seamlessly combining narrative, vivid description, scenes of desperate conflict, suspense, and an ironic patterning of events and characters. He wrote many compelling stories about his creatures' instinctive struggle for survival in a universe governed by elemental natural forces, chance, or the intervention of humans. In redefining plot to accommodate a world where cause and effect are ruled not by motivation and fate but by chance and instinct, he broke new ground. He also showed an uncanny ability to arouse empathy for the drama of life in the wild, a feat that was partly achieved by interpreting and dramatizing animal behaviour in human terms. In such stories as 'When Twilight Falls on the Stump Lots', about the victorious attack of a she-cow on a bear, 'The Last Barrier', a biography of a salmon, and 'The Little Tyrant of the Burrows', in which a greedy mole-shrew hunts and feeds voraciously for several pages before he too is polished off by a fox, this technique is restrained. But the task of creating hundreds of plots sometimes led Roberts to impart a 'psychology' to animal characteristics, in which greed, anger, hate, and revenge are read into their physical attributes or behaviour. Eyes are given human expressiveness:

> But the most thoroughly nightmarish feature about the whole unspeakable monster [a white squid] was the eyes. They were two vast concave lenses of inky blackness, bulging, and so high that their upper rims almost met at the top of the head. Absolutely lidless, and of an unfathomable malignancy, they looked as if nothing could be hidden from their awful gaze. ('In the World of the Ghost Light')

Roberts' first animal story, 'Do Seek Their Meat from God', is about a man who sets out to rescue his neighbour's child from hungry panthers and discovers that he has saved his own boy's life. The narrator asserts that 'It would be thoughtless superstition to say the beasts were cruel. . . . They were but seeking with the strength, the cunning, the deadly swiftness given them to that end, the food convenient for them'—in this case the boy. The dead panther cubs, discovered at the story's end, are the price paid for the boy's life. The intention here is to overturn received notions of animal barbarity and human civilization. Other stories balance human rapacity and greed (supposedly animal qualities) with animal dignity, as in 'The Lord of the Air', about the capture for a rich American of a kingly white-headed eagle and its triumphant escape. In stories where a human intervenes he is sometimes named Boy, and is less a character than a personification of the writer's 'pet theory' that the human animal is 'more competent as a mere animal than it gets the credit of being'. In the 'The Haunter of the Pine Gloom' the Boy is matched evenly with a pair of lynx or 'lucifees', whose depredation of farm animals arouses his 'primeval hunting instincts'. The story ends on a typically dispassionate note, describing the death of the female lynx in the Boy's trap—and ironic continuance. Another pattern of predation is evident in 'The Leader of the Run', where a salmon, seemingly the 'hero' of the story, is seized by a mink, who is subsequently robbed of his prey by an eagle. Ironic reversal and sudden death are repeated in 'The Sentry of the Sedge Flats', woven round a succession of deaths, united by the image of the butterfly; one butterfly is eaten by the heron at the story's beginning, and another alights on the dead body of the heron at the end.

A related contrast between animal and human worlds occurs in 'The Aigrette', where the focus is on the female of the human species—the coquette who needs a bird's plumage to complete her society image. Roberts relates this to the decimation of the egret colony, but he writes in a balanced manner that goes beyond the idea of conservation to achieve ironies of perception that invert preconceived notions of innocence and beauty in the world. Irony also appears in some of Roberts' story titles. For example, in 'A Treason of Nature' a play is made on the several meanings of the word 'nature'. In this story the luring of a bull moose by the hunter's moose call is an act of betrayal that the title suggests is itself a part of nature—man's nature being to hunt with intelligence and deception. But the story, as suggested by the title, offers more than this pragmatic view of the situation; tragic echoes of the word 'treason' remind the reader of the gap in the ranks of the wild left by this hunt. Roberts' use of irony marks his break with romantic nineteenth-century modes of perception and his entry into the ironic world of twentieth-century writing.

In the best of his animal stories, Roberts could set a scene and convey an atmosphere with succinct vividness: 'The windless grey-violet dusk, soft as mole's fur, brooded low over the bushy upland pasture.' Thus begins 'The Savage of the Dark', a story about a predatory owl. In pace, with its lingering vowels and multiple sets of adjectives, and in sound, with its variety of sibilants and soft labials, the sentence anticipates the story's contrast of softness and sudden savagery in the owl's attack, and reminds us that Roberts was also a poet.

This measured poeticism is absent, however, from some of Roberts' later stories where commercial urgency may have dictated speedy composition and a facile reliance on grandiose nineteenth-century diction. 'Leafage' and 'frondage' are much-used words, and overwritten effects, as in the opening of 'When Twilight Falls on the Stump Lots'—'. . . all seemed annointed, as it were, to an ecstasy of peace, by the chrism of that paradisal colour'—betray a mode of writing, soon dropped, that contrasts sharply with the crisp pragmatic tone of the story's ending.

Roberts' non-animal stories—for example, the Acadian stories in *By the Marshes of Minas* (1900)—suffer from over-reliance on the plot conventions of historical romance: love triumphs over the boundaries of historical enmity; young rebels are hidden by maidens from pursuit by the wicked Black L'Abbé; betwitchments, magic dwarfs, and talismanic jewels abound. These stories—unlike a great many of the animal stories—are best forgotten.

Ernest Thompson Seton (1860-1946) was born in England but spent his boyhood near Lindsay, Ontario, and in Toronto where, in the wilderness of the Don Valley, he had his first experiences of nature and animal life that led to his becoming a self-educated naturalist. In 1882 he moved to Manitoba (publishing *The Birds of Manitoba* in 1891) and in 1892 was appointed official naturalist for the province. In 1896 he moved permanently to the United States. The first of his many books of animal stories, *Wild Animals I Have Known*, was published in 1898. It contains his famous story 'Lobo, the King of Currumpaw', about the white wolf Blanca, who is trapped and killed, her mate Lobo, and his capture and death from (it is suggested) a broken heart. Not only are Seton's animal protagonists named by men ('Silverspot, the Story of a Crow' and 'Redruff, the Story of the Don Valley Partridge' are two other titles), but men feature largely in most of the stories. Even when human characters are peripheral (as in 'Silverspot'), the human presence is intrusively felt in the narrative voice, which is frequently first-person and didactic. Sometimes the human narrator is defensive: 'Those who do not know the animals well may think I have humanized them, but those who have lived so near them as to know somewhat of their ways and their minds will not think so.' ('Raggylug, the Story of a Cottontail Rabbit')

Despite Seton's defence, this narrative technique is less convincing than that of Roberts, who employs an invisible omniscient narrator and never finds it necessary to offer a plausible reason for his knowledge and understanding of events that happened far beyond human reach. Seton's concept of realism and of realistic presentation gave rise to almost diary-like chronicles of animal activity as seen through the eyes of man. But he took another step: he allowed the animals to express human responses and interpretations. This led him into the anomaly of 'translating' animal communication into English. 'Silverspot', for example, opens with an extensive catalogue of crow sounds, accompanied by musical notation and English 'translation'. One caw is said to mean 'Great danger—a gun, a gun, scatter for your lives.' The narrator of 'Raggylug' excuses this convention with these words: '. . . though in telling this story I freely translate from rabbit into English, *I repeat nothing that they did not say.*' In the introduction to *Wild Animals I Have Known*, Seton states: 'These stories are true. Although I have left the strict line of historical truth in many places, the animals in this book were all real characters. They lived the lives I have depicted, and showed the stamp of heroism and personality more strongly by far than it has been in the power of my pen to tell.' Roberts the literary artist, who does not insist on the veracity of his accounts, paradoxically creates a greater illusion of accuracy and immediacy in his animals, and conjures up a greater imaginative whole. His stories are therefore more compelling—and in essence more realistic—than Seton's, whose romanticized narratives are redolent of the popular magazine story that tugs at the reader's heartstrings and appeals to conventional wisdom. After the death of Raggylug's mother, Molly Cottontail, we are told that she was 'a true heroine' who 'fought a good fight in the battle of life'. She was 'good stuff; the stuff that never dies. For flesh of her flesh and brain of her brain was Rag. She lives in him, and through him transmits a fine fibre to her race.' Nevertheless Seton's best stories produce in the reader an easy acceptance of his conventions.

Unlike his contemporaries Roberts and Seton, **William Alexander Fraser** (1857-1933) wrote animal stories that were firmly rooted in ancient conventions. Born in Nova Scotia, he spent much of his life in Georgetown, Ont., and Toronto writing short stories and novels. The narratives in *Mooswa and Others of the Boundaries* (1900) and *The Sa-Zada Tales* (1905) are influenced by Scripture, in their biblical cadence and in such features as the patriarchal moose and the covenant embodied in the 'Law of the Boundaries'; and by Aesopian and Chaucerian patterns of plot and characterization—which contain nothing that was not in Chaucer's *The Parliament of Fowls*. There are echoes, too, of the recently published *Jungle Books* (1894, 1895) of Kipling. Fraser's animals are given personalities; all talk, all feel emotion; they hold councils and choose kings; and the 'Law of the Boundaries', which regulates the animals' predatory activities, denies the realities of carnivorous existence. But the animals' otherwise realistic behaviour, and the accurately rendered Canadian environment—Fraser makes liberal use of Indian animal names (*mooswa*, the moose; *muskwa*, the bear, *carcajou*, the wolverine) and of accurately described but generalized settings ('the Muskeg lands lying between the Saskatchewan River, the Arctic Ocean, and the Rocky Mountains')— endow his stories with a persuasive verisimilitude. They hold one's interest; as with Seton, the reader willingly accepts the conventions Fraser adhered to.

Other contemporaries of Roberts and Seton were **Edward William Thomson** (1894-1924) and Gilbert Parker, who churned out the kind of formulaic narratives that were popular in the nineteenth century. Thomson was a political journalist for the Toronto *Globe* from 1878 to 1901, and then spent ten years in Boston as 'revising editor' of *Youth's Companion*, a popular weekly magazine that published many of his stories, beginning with 'Petherick's Peril', which won the magazine's story competition in 1886. *Old Man Savarin Stories: Tales of Canada and Canadians* (1895) contained seventeen stories ('Petherick's Peril' was added to a 1917 reprint) that exhibit an ambitious array of settings and plots. Three are about Canadians in the American Civil War, one is set in the Boer War, several (replete with dialects) are set in French Canada and in Glengarry—for example his best-known story, 'The Privilege of the Limits', which was first published in *Harper's Weekly* in 1891. Eight of them are presented as told by an old man to a younger one—as in 'Petherick's Peril', about the terror experienced on a cliff face. This story demonstrates an ability to convey human psychology under conditions of great stress. Thomson's narrator makes palpable the terror of the climber, deftly balancing physical and psychological tensions. 'Miss Minnely's Management' spoofs Thomson's experience on the *Youth's Companion*. It is about George Renwick, an Improving Editor on *The Family Blessing,* who 'substituted "limb" for "leg", "intoxicated" for "drunk", and "undergarment" for "shirt" ' in the short story he was editing. 'When he should have eliminated all indecorum it would go to Miss Minnely [the owner], who would "elevate the emotional interest".' Though Thomson had a journalistic facility with narrative, his banal, unfelt language prevents his stories from coming to life.

The first book by **Gilbert Parker** (1862-1932)—who was born in Ontario but spent most of his life in England—was *Pierre and His People*, a collection of stories that had first appeared in the New York *Independent*. Published in London in 1892, it became popular and was reprinted many times; but Parker turned thereafter to writing historical novels of romance and adventure (many of them set in New France) that made him famous. The *Pierre* stories, colourful adventure tales set in the Canadian Northwest (which Parker never visited), are loosely linked by the vagrant figure of Pretty Pierre—half-breed, gambler, outlaw, and unlikely hero. Pierre's relationship to some of the stories is purely incidental; other characters have as good a claim to unify the collection—Shon McGann, for example. But Pierre—possibly derived from Bret Harte's Jack Hanlon (*Tales of the Argonauts*, 1875)—typifies the romantic frontier nature of the tales, whose plots lean heavily on the patterns of romance: what is lost is found; what was renounced is restored; honour triumphs even among thieves; outlaws repent and join the Riders of the Plains. One notable feature of Parker's stories is his use of interpolated songs. The tendency of his characters to burst into spontaneous song, expressing emotion or atmosphere, places Parker's stories firmly in the loose nineteenth-century convention of the sketch or anecdote. Parker never attempted the more rigid form of the modern short story.

Worthy of mention are two women short-story writers of the 1880s, each of whom wrote one story that appears in contemporary anthologies. The literary reputation of **Isabella Valancy Crawford** (1850-87) rests on her narrative poems (*Old Spookses' Pass, Malcolm's Katie, and Other Poems*, 1884), which she gloried in infusing with melodrama, colourful diction, and visual imagery. But she also wrote stories to support herself precariously—in an era of magazine publishing that created an insatiable demand for romantic fiction of whatever quality—and was published in Toronto, Montreal, and New York (in the popular magazines of Frank Leslie). Seven were collected in *Selected Stories of Isabella Valancy Crawford* (1975), edited by Penny Petrone. They reveal an amateurish command of structure, an extreme artificiality of language in narrative and dialogue, and a penchant for romantic twaddle. In 'A Five O'Clock Tea' Miss Trellais gives up her fiancé to the girl he really loves—and promptly dies, for reasons that are not entirely clear ('Whom the gods love die young'). The one story by Crawford that is anthologized is 'Extradited' (first published in the Toronto *Globe* in 1886), about a surprisingly devious young wife and mother. Silently contemptuous of her unlettered husband, she is nevertheless jealous of his friendship with the noble hired man, hiding out from the law, whom she secretly betrays—for a reward that fate denies her. In spite of a ragged narrative and Crawford's infelicitous way with words—for example, the husband's dialogue is marred by an awkward attempt to convey an Irish brogue—the dramatic intentions of the plot and the characterization of the wife (the men are mere stereotypes) are memorable.

The genre of romantic local-colour fiction had a much more able practitioner in **Susie Frances Harrison** (1859-1935), who became the author of two novels and several collections of verse. Her first book, however, was a collection of eleven stories, *Crowded Out! and Other Sketches*, published in 1886 under the pseudonym 'Seranus'. Many of them are about Englishmen who visit Canada, or English immigrants, and are narrated with a rather affected and unconvincing English voice; some have French-Canadian settings and characters, whose speech is conveyed in broken English. The title story—the shortest—is the first-person narrative of an over-wrought, frustrated Canadian writer in London who tries to publish stories with Canadian content there and despairs of success or of being able to return to his beloved in Canada. Harrison was able to convey—subtly, through gesture or demeanour—the psychological states of many of her characters, and she set the stage for her stories effectively. 'The Idyl of the Island', perhaps her best story, is about the chance encounter of an English visitor to Canada, Admiral Amherst, and a young Canadian woman. It opens with a detailed description of 'an exquisitely lovely island' in a lake lying 'midway between parallels 48 and 49 of latitude . . . in the northern hemisphere of the New World. . . . This island might seem just the size for two, and there were two on it on a certain July morning at five o'clock.' This is the prelude to a chaste but emotional hour-long meeting, leading to kisses, and a willed separation that precedes the appearance of the woman's husband, 'stout and pleasant and mild of countenance', returning in a row-boat from fishing. The smooth assurance and attempt at sophistication with which Harrison relates this romantic 'idyl' would be seen again (and improved upon), a few years later, in the stories of Sara Jean-nette Duncan.

Against this background of sentimental writing, *In the Village of Viger* (1896) by **Duncan Campbell Scott** (1862-1947) marks the first real break with the popular genres of romance, the frontier tale, and the local-colour story. Scott—who had a long career as a civil servant with the Indian Branch of the federal government, where he remained for over fifty years—is best known as a poet. He (along with Roberts) was one of the four Confederation Poets who, born in the 1860s and first published in the 1880s and 1890s, were the leading poets of the new Dominion. His Viger stories are set in a Quebec village, but they avoid the nostalgic timelessness of folksy Quebec tales because Viger is fixed in place and time. Though securely anchored in the outskirts of a big city, it allows its inhabitants to pursue an almost pastoral way of life—which is threatened by urbanization and changing times. The volume's introductory poem—'Whoever has from toil and stress / Put into ports of idleness . . . / Might for an hour his worry staunch, / In pleasant Viger by the Blanche'—suggests an idyllic setting, but the stories themselves ironically contradict its pastoral imagery, with new roads invading the fields, widows commuting to the city to work, and the rumble of streetcars disturbing the quiet environment.

This underlying sense of changing times strengthens the realism of Scott's stories and suggests the influence of French writers, such as Flaubert and de Maupassant, rather than American writers of magazine fiction. (Seven Viger stories, however, appeared in *Scribner's Magazine*.) But Scott did not disdain the older popular fictional forms. Some stories abound in sentiment: 'The Bobolink' resembles the moral stories of E.W. Thomson and Nellie McClung. The folk-tale motif anchors 'The Pedler' and other stories; and a Poe-like hint of the supernatural hangs over 'The Tragedy of the Seigniory', in which a phantom dog heralds tragic events. What lifts the volume as a whole above the limitations of individual stories is the sense of unity and sustained atmosphere provided by a common setting, strong characterization, and the quiet, ironic commentary.

The original edition of *In the Village of Viger* contained ten stories. (The New Canadian Library edition of 1973 adds seven more, drawn from *The Witching of Elspie* (1923), Scott's second story collection, and *The Circle of Affection* (1947), which contains stories along with poems and essays.) One of the links in the stories is Madame Laroque, the village gossip, who appears in 'The Little Milliner', 'The Wooing of Monsieur Cuerrier', 'The Pedler', and 'Paul Farlotte'. Whether as a main or peripheral character, Madame serves as an ironic touchstone of village opinion. As gull and buffoon (especially in 'The Wooing') she may owe something to older stock characters of comedy, though Scott updates that tradition by providing her with ironic commentaries.

A more important connecting link, however, is the concentration on changing times—a theme new to the Canadian short story. Scott focuses on the very act of change itself. Many characters are caught at turning-points in their lives, where they must choose (the choice is seldom a moral one, or free) between an old way and a new. Most take the necessary path, as in 'Josephine Labrosse', where the village girl is poised between two men: a city clerk and a woodsman. This story well documents the desperation of lone women and the pathetic decline from the respectable old-world ways of support—shopkeeping, letting rooms—to the vulgar new ways of earning a living, such as clerking in the city. Here, as in 'Paul Farlotte', the industrialization of Viger's world, which impinges unfavourably on the domestic realities of vulnerable women, brings out their strengths. They show quiet resourcefulness in finding new protectors, often in unconventional kinds of male-female relationships. 'No. 68 rue Alfred de Musset' stoops to melodrama as Eloise declares, 'I know I'll do something desperate . . . I must live; I was made to', and uses deception to begin her career as an adventuress. The little milliner and Marie St Denis in 'Paul Farlotte' create for themselves other more realistic ways of surviving in a male world.

The pressure of time and change on the most vulnerable part of the community also helps to set the book apart from other collections of Quebec tales. But in characterization too Scott is years ahead of his Canadian contemporaries. He makes his characters recognizably French Canadian not by means of dialect (as Thomson did in *Old Man Savarin Stories*) but with such details as French names, swear words, and song titles, as well as with delicate evocations of place and religious belief. (Even in his non-French-

Canadian stories, such as those from the 'MS. Journal of Archibald Muir', the Scots accent of Muir and his assistants at the trading-post is rendered in sentence structure and word choice and with the occasional 'Aye', rather than in quaint spellings and idiosyncratic grammar.)

Also notable is Scott's ability to suggest complex psychological states in a manner never equalled by Parker, and only occasionally by Thomson (as in 'Petherick's Peril'). Scott's Archibald Muir stories, set in a frontier trading-post, are marked by their carefully crafted narrative point of view, that of a dour Scotsman who conceals his emotions from all, including himself, while unwittingly exposing them to the reader between the lines. Through this naïve, self-revealing narrator Scott gives an ironic perspective to the much-anthologized 'Labrie's Wife' (*The Witching of Elspie*), a story of unreturned passion and mulish blindness that is introduced simply as 'an excerpt from the manuscript journal of Archibald Muir, clerk of the Honourable Hudson's Bay Company'.

Scott's mastery of psychological realism is also evident in his treatment of abnormal mental states. In 'The Desjardins', one of the Viger stories, Charles Desjardin inherits his father's insanity and imagines himself to be Napoleon Bonaparte. In two of the Muir stories, 'Vengeance is Mine' and 'In the Year 1806' (*The Witching of Elspie*), Scott explores, with much more sophistication, the impact of silence and solitude on the precarious mental balance of northern traders. In both stories tension builds between two men forced by circumstances into a stifling intimacy, and finally into madness. The latter story has a 'twist'; the reader first enters, then is abruptly released from, the madman's world of reality—a technique reminiscent of Ambrose Bierce's 'The Occurence at Owl Creek Bridge' (1891).

In presenting character as dynamic rather than static, as something shaped by social, temporal, and geographical realities, Scott moved towards what has been called the 'great modern subject', the disintegration of the human personality and consciousness. Another indication of his modernity is the concreteness of the settings for his stories. Fully six out of the ten in the Viger collection centre on a particular house in the village, about which a detailed description is built up collectively. (Such mapping of the commonplace location would later become the hallmark of a certain kind of American realism, best represented by Sherwood Anderson's *Winesburg, Ohio*, 1919.) This approach might have been influenced by the work of Sarah Orne Jewett, the Maine writer whose stories in *Scribner's* focused on a small rural town and particularly on the character and plight of women in such a setting. Scott shared with Jewett a conviction that the ordinary and the trivial were worthy of examination and could be shown to have significance. The Viger collection is remarkable for the sustained detachment of its presentation, the whole framed by an ironic relationship between the lives and troubles of its characters and the pastoral poem in the epigraph. This stance was later adopted, and exaggerated, by Leacock in *Sunshine Sketches*. But satire was *not* Scott's intention, nor would it be an important strand in the later development of the Canadian short story. What Scott achieved— almost alone—was a shrewd, measured, tolerant narrative voice dedicated to recording faithfully small people and smaller details of their lives. It neither submerges itself in the common events nor elevates itself too knowingly above them, and is always open to revelations of meaning and beauty.

Sara Jeannette Duncan (1861-1922), born in Brantford, Ontario, had a career as a journalist in Washington, Toronto, Montreal, and Ottawa before she married in 1890 and settled with her husband in Calcutta and then Simla, India. Though primarily a novelist, she produced one collection of four stories—*The Pool in the Desert* (1903; reprinted by Penguin in 1979)—three of which are long and divided into chapters. Heavily influenced by Henry James, she built her sophisticated stories on a given situation, but their style also owes much to her journalism—her columns, articles, and travel sketches in which she developed an unerring eye for the significant detail in a foreign landscape—which probably also contributed to her crisp narrative voice.

The voice in these stories is that of an intelligent, independent, penetrating female: critical, appreciative, and above all alive. (The male narrator of 'An Impossible Ideal' is an exception.) This tone sharpens the ironic contrast between mother and daughter in 'A Mother in India', where the daughter, reared in England, falls impossibly short of her mother's ideals of spirited womanhood. Passion and thought have all been squeezed out of young Cecily Farnham. Her mother blames this defect on her daughter's English upbringing, but the reader sees that the cause is at least partly the separation from her parents at an early age—a subject on which the mother steadfastly deludes herself. 'An Impossible Ideal' is about artistic and social conformity in the Anglo-Indian society of Simla and the artist's need for freedom. The male narrator—who, it can be admitted, does not sound like a man but like Duncan herself—begins the story by introducing peripherally the American painter Ingersoll Armour (who eventually flees Simla for a more receptive environment):

> To understand how we prized him, Dora Harris and I, it is necessary to know Simla. I suppose people think of that place, if they ever do think of it, as an agreeable retreat in the wilds of the Himalayas where deodars and scandals grow, and where the Viceroy if he likes may take off his decorations and go about in flannels. I know how useless it would be to try to give a more faithful impression, and I will hold back from the attempt as far as I can. Besides, my little story is itself an explanation of Simla. Ingersoll Armour might have appeared almost anywhere else without making social history. He came and bloomed among us in the wilderness, and such and such things happened. It sounds too rude a generalization to say that Simla is a wilderness; I hasten to add that it is a waste as highly cultivated as you like, producing many things more admirable than Ingersoll Armour. Still he bloomed there conspicuously alone.

Such a tone of knowing sophistication in the voice of a Canadian writer—which in Duncan is self-consciously worldly—was entirely new and would not be heard again until Ethel Wilson began publishing in the late 1930s, to be followed in the 1970s by Margaret Atwood.

2

CONSOLIDATION

The first Canadian short-story anthology, *Canadian Short Stories*, was published in 1928 by Macmillan of Canada and edited by **Raymond Knister** (1899-1932). A young writer of short stories himself (though he excluded himself from the collection), Knister had assiduously explored the whole field before arriving at his selection of seventeen stories, providing at the end of his book two appendixes that throw light on the work to date of Canadian writers in this genre. He lists 280 stories by 112 writers that had been published in books and magazines; and 47 authors who had published 91 collections of their own stories. Knister's introductory essay (bearing the same title as this book) is a kind of apologia for the lack of originality, and the adherence to commercial conventions prescribed by magazine publication, that had mainly characterized the Canadian short story. There were of course exceptions, which Knister recognized and included: E.W. Thomson's 'The Privilege of the Limits' (1891), the earliest story in the collection; Stephen Leacock's 'The Great Election in Missinaba County' from *Sunshine Sketches* (1912); and a late animal story by Charles G.D. Roberts, 'A Gentleman in Feathers' (1924). Duncan Campbell Scott—to whom the book is dedicated and whose first collection, *In the Village of Viger* (1896), Knister says had made 'the most satisfying individual contribution to the Canadian short story'—is represented by 'Labrie's Wife' from *The Witching of Elspie* (1923). Several writers are included who are still known—but not as short-story writers: Merrill Denison, Norman Duncan,

Marjorie Pickthall, Mazo de la Roche, and Alan Sullivan. They were included with six writers who are not at all known today—for example, Will E. Ingersoll ('The Man Who Slept Till Noon', 1918), who receives special mention by Knister. The stories by all these secondary writers are skilful and readable, but in Knister's words— describing the majority of recent Canadian stories—they also seem 'mechanical', and in expressing 'the roots of a nation's life' have 'the aroma of wax and paper'. Of the 'new' writers in Knister's anthology, only Morley Callaghan—whose 'Last Spring They Came Over' (1929) opens the collection and continues to be an- thologized—has had a lasting reputation.

In Knister's own stories rejection of the planned, formulaic plot, and of over-obvious technique, led to a relatively plotless story. At- mosphere and nuance dominate his stories of farm life in South- western Ontario, which frequently centre on a young, sensitive protagonist and his or her emerging awareness of the beauty and pain of the immediate world, and the promise of the wider one beyond the farm. The strongest qualities of his stories—charac- terization through dialogue and action; strong evocation of locality—are achieved not simply by describing the physical, but also by conveying values and beliefs; by the creative use of am- biguity; and by employing quiet revelatory endings. All these qualities stem from his rejection of plot.

Ambiguity is the distinctive feature of the long, seemingly ram- bling 'Peaches, Peaches', which depicts harvest activities in a peach orchard through the eyes of young Ed Burkin. The story focuses on Ed's growing awareness of sexual undercurrents in his relations with the country girls employed as pickers and, surprisingly, in the electricity that charges the contacts of his respectable sister-in-law, Eleanor, with the hired man. Young Ed is both aware and not aware. By concentrating on the little half-formed thoughts glimpsed in the corners of Ed's mind that only later will assume significance, Knister captures feelings in a state of flux.

In some of Knister's stories—'The Loading', for example—am- biguity merely manages to confuse the reader. In others, such as 'The First Day of Spring', Knister seems unwilling to confront the story's evocative indefiniteness. But the finely wrought 'Elaine'

(published in the Paris magazine *This Quarter* in 1925) successfully draws the reader once more into the world of 'Peaches,
Peaches'—the adolescent world of half-knowledge and its conse-
quent pain. On the train to high-school in the city, young Elaine
Wilks suffers agonies of embarrassment at her mothers' seeming
indifference to the social snubs around her.

A good example of Knister's control of tone and atmosphere at
the end of his stories occurs in 'The First Day of Spring'. The young
narrator has just been stripped of his cherished illusions about a girl
from a neighbouring farm, through his father's revelation of her
disgrace and exile. In the light of this new knowledge, the boy listens to the singing of the girl next door:

> From across the fields the light hidden voice came reaching again and
> then it stopped, as though for an answer. The air was chill, and with the
> darkness winter seemed to be returning.
> After a few minutes I moved away toward the barn. In the gloom of
> the stable I stroked the warm nose of a colt. 'You're going to be broken
> in,' I whispered. He was strangely quiet.

Not all of Knister's stories exhibit this quiet ability to register
change and growth through control of tone. Less effective than his
farm stories are his gangster stories set in Chicago (where Knister
lived briefly in 1924), especially 'Hackman's Night', the most
reliant on plot. 'Innocent Man', a longer story of a naïve youth
caught up for a night in the jail system of Chicago, is better precise-
ly *because* it eschews plot and creates a nightmarish atmosphere
through dialogue and claustrophobic setting. Occasionally
Knister's stories drift close to sentimentality, as in 'Lilacs for First
Love', and sometimes flirt disastrously with a clumsy humour
('Horace and the Haymow')—in stories written for popular
magazines. Knister's major weakness, however, was caused by a
serious disability that affected his style: he had no ear for language
and syntax. He used ponderous, multi-syllabled diction
('innumerable', 'immeasurable', 'unevadable', 'impenetrable',
'immanent') and clumsy phrasings that fail disastrously to achieve
the desired effect: 'His father's call struck a surprise in him . . .'
from 'Mist-Green Oats'. This example of his farm stories is also

marred by heavy abstract nouns that clutter the style, obscure the meaning, and cloud the voice of the narrator: 'Already he began to miss her [his mother]. Nearly two days were gone. But he should have, though only until realization, for expectance the last one of her absence.' It is curious that 'Mist-Green Oats' should appear so often in anthologies, since it is by far the worst offender in the matter of style.

A man of wide reading in contemporary literature who unfortunately died young, Knister had ambitions as a writer of 'significant' stories that were thwarted by his technical shortcomings. His serious literary interests placed him (like Callaghan, whom he knew) in sad isolation in the Canada of the time, yet he nevertheless achieved a place in our literary history as an earnest striver in several genres. Some of his stories have been collected by Michael Gnarowski in *Selected Stories of Raymond Knister* (1972) and by Peter Stevens in *The First Day of Spring: Stories and Other Prose* (1976).

Morley Callaghan (b.1903) succeeded where Knister failed. Callaghan (along with Ernest Hemingway) purged the literary and latinate from his diction to forge a simple and direct form of expression for the short story. Like Knister, Callaghan was first published in *This Quarter*, an achievement that signalled that the stories of both young men were serious, contemporary, experimental, and exciting. Callaghan's 'A Girl With Ambition', which appeared in the Winter 1926 issue, was revolutionary in its choice of subject, setting, style, and structure. In this story, about an attractive but uneducated girl who dreams of 'getting on' in the world, he exhibited a modernist fascination with the ordinary and the everyday. Most of Callaghan's characters are working people, though there is a sprinkling of pool-players, gamblers, and bums, along with prosperous lawyers, insurance brokers, and bank managers. There are no heroes, no people elevated above others or distinguished by extraordinary abilities. His Ediths and Effies, Harolds and Bills, are almost aggressively ordinary, and usually city-dwellers. Callaghan makes the city the new territory for Canadian short fiction. This choice—perhaps owing to his early stint as a reporter for the Toronto *Star*—marks a great departure from the half-pastoral of Scott's stories, the Empire settings of Sara Jeannette Duncan, or even the rural-Ontario idylls of Knister.

Like Knister, Callaghan had a contemporary interest in human psychology, but approached emotion from the inside in order to make his reader feel not the names but the nuances of the human dilemmas he described. Whereas Knister tended to pinpoint emotion with all the precise latinate adjectives and abstract nouns at his command, creating a case study rather than a character, Callaghan adopted an unemotional style and rejected almost all linguistic clichés, disdaining even the word 'love'. He developed instead a palette of simple adjectives—fine, good, easy, large, bright, strong, quick, lively, slow, eager—and varied them to capture all nuances of appearance and emotion. Love in Callaghan's stories is rarely more than half articulated, usually as a 'strong feeling', and lust appears as an 'eager' or a 'restless' feeling. This technique, which was appropriate for the inarticulate nature of his characters, brings the reader close to the actual experiences of the ordinary and un-educated people he often wrote about as they struggle with half-understood motives and desires.

The simplicity of Callaghan's style extends to syntax as well as diction. He frequently uses short declarative sentences, anchored wherever possible by copulative verbs, or by the plainest, punchiest action verbs—go, come, do, put, ask, look—and incorporates the idioms and rhythms of everyday speech into the narrative voice. These techniques are apparent in a typical opening passage (from 'Their Mother's Purse', *The New Yorker*, 1936):

> Joe went around to see his mother and father, and while he was talking with them and wondering if he could ask for the loan of a dollar, his sister Mary, who was dressed to go out for the evening, came into the room and said, 'Can you let me have fifty cents tonight, Mother?'
> She was borrowing money all the time now, and there was no excuse for her, because she was a stenographer and made pretty good pay. It was not the same with her as it was with their older brother, Stephen, who had three children, and could hardly live on his salary.

Here Callaghan wastes no time on setting; his style *is* the setting, and he sketches it in with his direct, yet casual, approach to the subject of the loan, in a world where money and its lack is a daily preoccupation. In the second paragraph the narrative voice slips easily into accommodation with Joe's point of view, as the idiom 'pretty good pay' gives us the ordinary tenor of Joe's thoughts.

Callaghan's pared-down style is frequently associated with Ernest Hemingway's. The two writers met—in Toronto in 1923, and later in Paris—and Callaghan may have picked up some stylistic influence from the older and more forceful American, who acted as his literary mentor in Europe. It is more likely, however, that both were struggling separately towards a style appropriate to the twentieth-century experience as they saw it, and stumbled on a similar approach to documenting very different views of the world. For Hemingway, the twentieth century was a time when the death of meaning resulted in radical fragmentation on a cultural level and terrible isolation on the personal. For Callaghan it was notable for the mute struggle of individual souls towards some kind of personal salvation.

Callaghan lacks Hemingway's sure touch with dialogue. His narrative voice is most often used to sketch in the background of emotions, involvements, and the tangled web of personal history that Hemingway can hint at in the terse dialogue that forms the tip of his fictional 'iceberg'. Callaghan further differs from Hemingway in sometimes opting for a more closed ending to his stories, achieving in their completeness the 'well-made' magazine story that descends from O. Henry and de Maupassant. Predictable endings characterize his feebler stories, such as 'Silk Stockings' (*The New Yorker*, 1932), 'Magic Hat', and 'The Lucky Lady'.

More often, however, Callaghan's stories are open-ended, and his final paragraphs leave the reader and the characters with conflicting surges of deep feeling. For example, at the end of 'Sister Bernadette' (*Scribner's Magazine*, 1932) the stern nun clutches an abandoned baby, overwhelmed by half-understood longings:

> Sister Bernadette began to think of herself as a young girl again. For the first time in years she was disturbed by dim, half-forgotten thoughts: 'Oh, why do I want so much to keep this one baby? Why this one?' her soul, so chaste and aloof from the unbridled host swarming nightly in the city streets, was now overwhelmed by a struggle between something of life that was lost and something bright and timeless within her that was gained. But she started to tremble all over with more unhappiness than she had ever known. With a new, mysterious warmth, she began to

hug the child that was almost hidden in her heavy black robes as she pressed it to her breast.

It is characteristic of Callaghan's technique and his moral purpose to leave this story at a point not of culmination but of new departure where the future of Sister Bernadette seems to open out before her, not as a simplistic golden path to happiness-ever-after, but as the ordinary human path of struggle between what has been lost and the 'bright and timeless' thing that has been gained. One of his best endings occurs in 'This Man My Father', an excellent story in which Joe, the rising young New York executive, becomes reacquainted with his ageing, provincial father:

> When he smiled like that I felt him walking beside me; I felt that mystery of having been close to the boyhood of a man who was now old and who was sitting beside me smiling at me. I had seen the innocence of his childhood restored to him for a little while. As I kept looking at him the restless excitement and wonder were growing in me. I had a great hunger to know of the things that had delighted him, the things he had hoped for when he was a kid far away in London and happy, before he ever thought of Canada or heard of Windsor—this man, my father, whom I had found walking down near the Fulton Street fish market.

As these open endings suggest, Callaghan's subject is the human heart, and his plot is usually an interior one. When the twists and turns of fate demanded by the well-made story occasionally appear in his short fiction (for example, with the loss of the cap in 'A Cap for Steve', *Esquire*, 1952), they are meant to illuminate an interior struggle. Character in these stories is never one-dimensional, for Callaghan captures the moment when conflicting motives surface. His characters can be both jealous and loving ('The Consuming Fire', *Harper's Bazaar*, 1938; 'Watching and Waiting', *Redbook*, 1936), selfish and giving ('Let Me Promise You', *Esquire*, 1933), cruel and tender ('The Blue Kimono', *Harper's Bazaar*, 1935). Callaghan's small dramas of the human spirit suggest his vision of an infinitely divided human nature, bathed in a light of understanding, that implies acceptance on our part, if not forgiveness.

Also notable is Callaghan's ingenious use of urban landscape to create non-standard symbols and new structural metaphors that become, through context, immediately comprehensible. In 'A Girl with Ambition' he establishes poles of moral and social reference, with the chorus line at the La Plaza Hotel at one end of Toronto, and the district of businessmen and lawyers at the other; his young lovers meet on the middle ground at a department store, Eaton's. Young Harry, a law student, is merely marking time at Eaton's; Mary, on the other hand, imagines that she is on her way up from the chorus line. Their lives converge for a moment at the mid-point of their society's definition of financial and moral respectability. In another story, 'An Escapade', Callaghan uses a Toronto theatre and a Toronto cathedral as *loci* on a grid of changing urban values. He repeatedly evokes the real, ordinary places of the city to create a symbolically charged personal landscape against which the moral dramas of his characters are played out.

The well-known 'Now That April's Here' has few characteristics of the typical Callaghan story (though the spare, unemotional style and skilful construction are very much in evidence). This may be because it originated as a challenge from an editor, when Callaghan was in Paris in 1929, to write a story about two fellow-Canadians, John Glassco and Graeme Taylor, who were drawing attention to themselves in Paris with their eccentric behaviour. Articulate and far from ordinary, entirely unlike the kind of people Callaghan usually wrote about, they are observed coolly from a distance—the narrator does not enter into their lives or interpret their feelings. But the detachment is not complete. The narrator betrays a not quite imperceptible aversion to the two young men, who are seen as trivial and of ambiguous sexuality—and are one-dimensional. The story was first published in *This Quarter* in 1929.

Callaghan began publishing his more than eighty short stories in an auspicious way, not only in *This Quarter* (1926) but also in the American magazine *Scribner's* (1928). His transatlantic début marks the beginning of an era in the history of Canadian literature when the short story became simultaneously serious and profitable, a twin recognition substantiated by European reception and American book publication. Scribner's became Callaghan's publisher, bringing out *A Native Argosy*, which included two novellas and short stories, in 1929. *Now That April's Here* followed in 1936. In the same year *The New Yorker* accepted 'The

Faithful Wife', the first of many stories by Callaghan to appear in that magazine. His later work appeared in such diverse magazines as *Harper's Bazaar*, *Esquire*, *Redbook*, and *Maclean's*. Callaghan inaugurated a wide publishing strategy that would later be perfected by Hugh Garner, a younger writer whose style owes a debt to Callaghan. A selection of Callaghan's stories appeared in 1959 from Macmillan, *Morley Callaghan's Stories*, which included most of the frequently anthologized stories and helped to define the canon. In 1985 an additional collection was published, *The Lost and Found Stories of Morley Callaghan*, comprising twenty-six stories omitted from the first collection, many of which are of high quality, and some of which (for example, 'An Enemy of the People' and 'This Man My Father') are among his very best.

Ethel Wilson (1888-1980) was a short-story writer of a slightly later period. Born in South Africa, she lived most of her life in Vancouver. Although older than both Callaghan and Knister, Wilson did not begin to publish her writing until she was middle-aged, her first story appearing in 1937 ('I Just Love Dogs', *The New Statesman*). Though her remaining twenty-or-so stories were all published in the forties and fifties, and collected in 1961 in *Mrs. Golightly and Other Stories*, they have what has been called an 'Edwardian' sensibility, and exist outside the mainstream of contemporary development in the short story. Wilson's stories, however, are clearly modernist in their ironic tone and their sophisticated control of narrative voice. Their innovative approach to first-person narration differentiates them in technique from anything before in the Canadian short story. Wilson employs a limited point of view to suggest multiple perspectives on events ('I Just Love Dogs') and multiple levels in the psychology of her characters ('Mrs. Golightly', 'Beware the Jabberwock . . .'), and a variety of settings: California ('Mrs. Golightly'), Egypt ('Haply the Soul of My Grandmother'), central Europe ('We Have to Sit Opposite'), Vancouver, and the interior of British Columbia.

Most of Wilson's stories explore the middle-class social life that Laura, in 'Truth and Mrs. Forrester', describes as 'a most peculiar erection built of imponderables and invisibles'. In making these social realities both palpable and visible, Wilson exhibits a delicate detachment from, and a fascination with, the idiosyncrasies of human behaviour. 'A Drink with Adolphus', which portrays multiple points of view, juxtaposes two highly incompatible responses to an evening party, conveying not only two characters' perceptions of each other but their vastly dissimilar approaches to the vagaries of life. The threat of potential violence that may lie behind a genteel exterior emerges briefly here, as it also does—more overtly—in what is perhaps Wilson's best story, 'The Window'. Here the 'great big window' reveals by day the unpeopled view from the living-room of Mr Willy, and by night becomes a mirror that not only reflects his sterile existence but conceals a figure of menace lurking in the dark. Using a backdrop of middle-class gentility, Wilson also ventures, in 'Mr. Sleepwalker', to represent abnormal states of mind. Like D.H. Lawrence and David Garnett before her, she employs animal motifs to construct a psychological fable that explores and externalizes deep-seated emotional reactions: Mary Manly, who for many years has been deprived of her husband's company and thus of the emotional sustenance she craves, becomes prey to an instinctual fear that is eventually embodied in a pervasive 'dank wild earthy smell of something old and unknown'—a smell that accompanies a series of terrifying encounters with the enigmatic, weasel-like Mr Sleepwalker. In another vein, 'From Flores' portrays both the savage beauty and the brutality of a Pacific storm in a story about the anxieties of ordinary people who are powerless to defend themselves against violence—in both nature and man.

Wilson was a highly polished writer, but she sometimes failed to convey a sense of felt experience, and occasionally her ironic dénouements seem contrived. Her voice sounds most authentic in ironic observations on middle-class behaviour and attitudes. The darkly humorous 'We Have to Sit Opposite', popular in anthologies, exemplifies her use of this astringent tone. A sense of menace, held at bay by the two young women's slightly hysterical hilarity, is underscored in the story's gnomic final sentence, with its grim historical allusion to the beginning of the Second World War:

> The two young women took care to sleep until the train reached Munich. Then they both woke up.

> Many people slept until they reached Munich. Then they all began to wake up.

In her well-known article 'A Cat Among the Falcons' (*Canadian Literature* No. 2, Autumn 1959), Wilson declared that writing can be learned—though it cannot be taught—and that most important is the achievement of an individual voice. This results from a moment of synthesis—an 'incandescence'—from which 'meaning emerges, words appear, they take shape in their order, a fusion occurs'. The calm, luminous surface of her own stories may well result from such an 'incandescence'.

Although **Hugh Garner** (1913-79) began his publishing career around the same time as Ethel Wilson, he belongs securely in the tradition of Callaghan, Hemingway, and numerous American artists of the hard-boiled style of writing. Deciding to try to earn his living as a writer after the Second World War, Garner became perhaps the most widely read short-story writer in Canada. His more than fifty stories appeared in almost every popular Canadian magazine—including *The Canadian Forum, Chatelaine, Saturday Night, The Canadian Home Journal*—and were also broadcast on CBC's 'Anthology' series. Taking wide exposure and prolific output a step further than Callaghan, he muscled himself into literary prominence and popularity. There is no doubt, however, that this success owed something to his true gifts as a storyteller. He has been lauded by critics as 'the best storyteller we have', and in stories pitting men against great natural dangers ('Red Racer', 'One Mile of Ice') he displays his formidable skill as a spinner of yarns.

For his subject matter Garner chose three main areas, two of which display especially well his talents as a tale-teller: his hobo and itinerant-worker stories ('Another Time, Another Place, Another Me', 'Hunky') and his stories of the Spanish Civil War ('How I Became an Englishman', 'The Stretcher Bearers'). In both Garner shows his obsession (the literary obsession of the thirties and forties) with social injustice, tyranny, and the plight of ordinary men caught in extraordinary world conditions. His third subject—city life in Toronto, Montreal, and Quebec—is perhaps most characteristic of his work, at least in popular and literary memory. Although some of his city stories (for example, 'A Trip for Mrs.

Taylor') are formulaic, replete with twist endings and clichéd characters, many capture the feel of the city as well as, if not better than, Callaghan's Toronto stories do. Like Callaghan, Garner extracted metaphor from the city landscape. In 'Our Neighbours the Nuns' the triple enclosure—the convent fence, the walls of the old city, and Quebec City itself—suggests the nuns' triple isolation from the twentieth-century world around them. Garner juxtaposes two different worlds—one Protestant, English, secular, active and mobile; the other Catholic, Gallic, spiritual, passive, and rooted in one spot in place and time—and, although his narrator compares the mendicant nuns to Robinson Crusoe, they actually pursue a very different course from Crusoe's vigorous, active Protestant accommodation of his material needs to his spiritual relationship with God. They are obliged to wait for donations, passively accepting the flotsam and jetsam of the twentieth century.

This story, unjustly neglected by critics and anthologists, epitomizes Garner's ability to create windows on reality, giving the reader a favoured glimpse of something rare. Also effective is the often-anthologized 'One-Two-Three Little Indians', about an Indian's inability to prevent the death of his child, which succeeds so well because it avoids pathos and melodrama and resolutely refuses to name villains. Other excellent stories are 'The Yellow Sweater' and 'The Conversion of Willie Heaps', which was included in *Best American Short Stories* for 1952.

Garner's stories—collected in *Hugh Garner's Best Stories* (1963), which won a Governor General's Award; *Men and Women* (1966); and *Violation of the Virgins* (1971)—are not uniformly good. Many display the taint of commercial production: facile clichéd endings, or clumsy plot twists to resolve the action. All too often Garner shows a tendency to over-articulate his symbolic scaffolding. Labouring to connect the title to the story, he often bars the door to other meanings, trapping the reader inside the narrow edifice of his fiction; stories such as 'The Father', 'Tea with Miss Mayberry', and 'The Nun With Nylon Stockings' are in this sense *too* well made. The plain style he employs is often quietly effective, as at the end of his excellent hobo story, 'Another Time, Another Place, Another Me': 'After a long wait a kitchen worker handed us each a tin plate of macaroni-and-cheese, and we squatted on our haunches in the yard and ate it. It sure tasted good.' Although the hard-boiled manner and even the grammar frequently become slapdash, Garner displays a gift for conveying a certain reality and a genuine empathy for the underdog, especially in 'Hunky' and 'E Equals MC Squared'. His popularity, and his handful of excellent stories, assure him a place in the history of the Canadian short story as a master storyteller—who was sometimes in need of a ruthless editor.

Only one of the stories ('Snow') of **Frederick Philip Grove** (1879-1948) was widely known during his lifetime, but he deserves mention here for his possible influence on subsequent writers of the prairie short story, such as Sinclair Ross and W. O. Mitchell. Best known for his ponderous novels with prairie settings, Grove also achieved some fame for *Over Prairie Trails* (1922), a collection of seven sketches with a Manitoban setting. These are not short stories but rather a set of linked meditative essays, occasioned by a repeated horse-and-buggy journey over rough rural territory. Heavy on description, as well as on philosophical and scientific observation, they document the route, its natural features and human habitations, and the role of this journey in the life of the schoolmaster-narrator. As the seasons change the route alters and presents varying challenges to man and horse, becoming a metaphor for the schoolmaster's progress through life. This type of carefully integrated philosophical exercise would not be repeated in Canadian short fiction until 1961 in Malcolm Lowry's 'The Forest Path to the Spring'.

Most of Grove's stories appear in *Tales from the Margin* (1971), based on a manuscript collection made and titled by Grove himself in 1929. Published first in 1926 and 1927 in the *Winnipeg Tribune Magazine*, many of them are really character sketches, or anecdotes—attempts to document the human types found in rural life. There is a flavour of literary sociology about Grove's portraits of typical people in stories such as 'The Spendthrift', 'The First Day of an Immigrant', 'The Agent', and 'The Dead-Beat'. Even more documentary in tone is his anatomy of the Depression and its effect on human lives in stories such as 'Relief' or 'Riders'. Grove's most widely reprinted story, 'Snow' (not to be confused with the sketch, also entitled 'Snow', in *Over Prairie Trails*), exhibits his skill at evoking the coldness and bleakness of the prairie winter, and its unforgiving relationship with human weakness. Sometimes Grove's narrative voice recalls that of Susanna Moodie and the early journal writers as it plays the role of translator, decoding the wilderness into civilized terms for European consumption:

> Towards morning the blizzard had died down, though it was still far from daylight. Stars without number blazed in the dark-blue sky which presented that brilliant and uncompromising appearance always characterizing, on the northern plains of America, those nights in the dead of winter when the thermometer dips to its lowest levels.

Beyond natural description, the power of the story about the death of Redcliff, a hapless prairie farmer, and his neighbours' search for the snow-covered sleigh and body, lies in its oblique narrative structure. The action begins far from the scene of the tragedy and drifts gradually up to it, borrowing some of its relentless motion from the blizzard it chronicles. Although it lays bare a simple and terrible tragedy of loss, the story ends on an affirmative note with the consolation of the widow and her family, showing Grove's belief in the power of human will and of collective action to overcome the worst natural obstacles.

Grove's naturalist fiction prefigures the later brand of prairie realism that Sinclair Ross would make his own. But Grove's prairie vision declares its allegiance to an earlier code in two significant ways. First, his stories still feature heroes and the possibility of heroic action. His Abe Carroll in 'Snow' stands above the other characters in intelligence, wealth, and calm resolve. He exudes a strength that can withstand the worst that the elements have to offer. But Grove also features the weak—men like Redcliff in 'Snow'— who necessarily fall victim to blizzards and other natural disasters. By the time the much-younger Ross began to write in the early 1930s the heroic figure had almost completely disappeared (existing only in the dreams of the young), and all men belonged to the gang of futility. The second old-fashioned feature of Grove's writing concerns his use of the prairie landscape. His almost scientific detachment in the description of natural phenomena (such as the effects of wind on snow) produces a vividness of realistic description that was unparalleled at the time. His scientific interest, however, often triumphs over his human interest: in Grove, snow is merely snow after all. It remained for Ross to perfect in his stories the use of landscape as a symbol—fusing man and prairie in interlocking metaphors.

Although **Sinclair Ross**'s short stories began appearing only seven or eight years after Grove's, Ross belonged to another generation in sensibility and style. Born in 1908, he was twenty-nine years younger than Grove, and only twenty-six when his first story ('No Other Way', 1934) appeared in *Queens' Quarterly*. His stories were not collected until much later, in *The Lamp at Noon and Other Stories* (1968) and *The Race and Other Stories* (1982).

Ross's chosen fictional territory, the Prairies, was a location that up to this point in Canadian fiction had usually signified a romanticized approach and the sentimental characters and endings of magazine fiction. (Grove's stories retain a flavour of this.) Ross focuses on the harsh reality of farm life in Saskatchewan on a bare and unforgiving land. His stories usually deal with two ruling conflicts: one between man and the elements of land and weather, and another between man and his own failure in human relationships. In his three best-known stories—'The Lamp at Noon', 'A Field of Wheat', and 'The Painted Door'—a male character, Paul or John, confronts his double failure: to subdue the land and make it fertile, and to achieve communication and communion with a wife who seems to have drifted away. These two kinds of failure seem connected because Ross uses the prairie landscape as a metaphor for—almost an externalization of—the territory of mind and soul. In this metaphor the borderline between the object described and the image used to describe it is blurred, since man and land mirror one another's stubborn, unyielding, tragic qualities. The strength of these three stories lies in their powerful evocation of solitary men and women lost in a vast inner and outer wilderness, a dilemma that is seemingly fated to crush life and spirit.

This debunking of the soft, romantic prairie myth creates a myth of its own—of the prairie as a place of trial, tragedy, and catharsis (one that would anchor the stories of later writers, such as W.O.

Mitchell). It is for this remaking of the prairie myth that Ross's stories are important, for they are conservative in technique and form. Only occasionally does Ross venture from a third-person into a retrospective first-person narrative voice, usually when telling the story of a young boy, as in 'The Outlaw', 'The Runaway', or 'Cornet at Night'—though in his short fiction no narrative voice sounds the delicate, ironic note of Mrs Bentley's journal entries in Ross's novel, *As For Me and My House* (1941). The style of the stories, however, is polished, with a controlled lyricism that leads to memorable, Conradian passages of natural description, such as that of the gathering storm in 'The Painted Door':

> Before her as she watched a mane of powdery snow reared up breast-high against the darker background of the stable, tossed for a moment angrily, and then subsided again as if whipped down to obedience and restraint. But another followed, more reckless and impatient than the first. Another reeled and dashed itself against the window where she watched.

One of the strengths of Ross's writing is his ability to find exact, concrete images for the dominant abstract motifs of isolation, loneliness, and deprivation—in the torn but cherished circus poster in 'Circus in Town'; in the lamp lit at midday against the dark of the dust storm in 'The Lamp at Noon'—but without Knister's over-blown phraseology. He makes an unusual use of the word 'clench', both as verb and noun, to evoke the closed-in, defiant, stubborn character of his male heroes, such as John in 'A Field of Wheat', who gambles all on one crop of wheat and on the fickle summer weather, while his wife, Martha, watches anxiously:

> Or perhaps it [the wheat] lived, perhaps the rain came, June, July, even into August, hope climbing, wish-patterns painted on the future. And then one day a clench and tremble to John's hand; his voice faltering, dull. Grasshoppers perhaps, sawflies or rust; no matter, they would grovel for a while, stand back helpless, then go on again.

Used with a negative prefix, the word captures Ross's vision of the possible release from spiritual and marital isolation, as in Martha's dream of a bright future of good crops: 'Three hundred acres ready to give perhaps a little of what it had taken from her—John, his love, his lips unclenched.'

Ross has a place in this maturing period in the Canadian short story because his work epitomizes its coming-of-age in style, form, voice, and subject. After 1968, when his stories were first collected in *The Lamp at Noon*, they immediately became a touchstone of quality in Canadian short fiction. In their relentless realism, their depiction of suffering, stoic humanity, and their attention to the land and climate of a recognizable and uniquely Canadian place, they conformed to the contemporary ideal of a Canadian short story. Appearing in the same year, Alice Munro's stories of Southwestern Ontario in *Dance of the Happy Shades* would be compared with those in *The Lamp at Noon* because they too explore the everyday trials and tragedy of ordinary people, but in a small-town setting rather than on the Prairies.

Other new writers of short stories appeared during the forties and fifties, some of whom were represented in Robert Weaver's and Helen James's anthology *Canadian Short Stories* (1952), containing stories that had been broadcast on the CBC. This anthology is important because it highlights the increasing role of the radio as a medium for popularizing the developing Canadian short story. Some of the twenty-four stories are by established writers—Hugh Garner, Sinclair Ross, Ethel Wilson—but many are by a new generation of writers emerging in the late forties and early fifties. Two from this group stand out: Joyce Marshall's 'The Old Woman' and James Reaney's 'The Bully'. Both stories blend realistic treatment of a rural locale with explorations into the psyche of their characters. **James Reaney** (b.1926), however, adds what would become a characteristic mythopoeic dimension to his story's amalgam of realistic detail and folkloric motif.

Although **Joyce Marshall** (b.1913) has not been a prolific writer of short stories—her one collection, *A Private Place*, was not published until 1975—the quality of her writing, with its precise control of the language of psychological suspense, is well represented by her early story 'The Old Woman'. An English war bride, Molly, joins her Canadian husband, only to find him changed, withdrawn, and suspicious. At their remote house by a paper mill she discovers that it is a machine and not a woman that has replaced her in Toddy's affections. Too long isolated in this remote place, he has come to worship what he calls 'the old woman', the turbines and dials of the electric power generator. Conflict exists not only between Molly and Toddy, but within Molly herself, as she tries to avoid acceptance of her husband's mental condition.

Reaney's 'The Bully'—about a similar psychological torture—is set in the southwestern Ontario locale that animates all of his later stories, poetry, and drama, and would soon provide material for Munro. The subtly drawn—and recognizably Ontarian—Canadian schoolboy who is the first-person narrator speaks in a forthright tone of engaging informality, evoking exact nuances of place and time:

> Every Saturday night we children all took turns bathing in the dish-pan and on Sundays, after Sunday-school, we would all sit out on the lawn and drink the lemonade that my father would make in a big glass pitcher. The lemonade was always slightly green and sour like the moon when it's high up in a summer sky.

Taunted by a loutish bully, the boy finally leaves school in despair, feigning expulsion for a minor infraction of school rules. The bully who has haunted his days returns in his dreams. Reaney gives the youth a folkloric trio of dreams, which together reveal the meaning of the bully—a meaning that is clear to the reader, but only dimly perceived by the boy himself; latent in the dream symbols, it waits for him to grow to understanding. In the dreams the bully, with his obscene remarks and taunts of babyhood, becomes the objectification of the boy's own fear of growing up—of its roles, responsibilities, and sexual complications. The third dream is Reaney's imaginative *tour de force* :

> There was a round pond there surrounded by a grove of young chokecherry trees. I pushed through these and came to the edge of the pond. There lay the Bully looking almost pitiful, his arms and legs bound with green ropes made out of nettles. He was drowned dead, half in the water and half out of it, but face up. And in the dim light of the dawn I knelt down and kissed him gently on the forehead.

The salutation to his nemesis becomes a gesture of ritual acknow-
ledgement and even identity.

These two stories, by Reaney and Marshall, reappeared eight
years later in Weaver's anthology in the World's Classics Series:
Canadian Short Stories (1960). While beginning with work by the
earliest Canadian short-story writers—Thomson, Roberts, Scott,
Leacock, Grove, Wilson, Knister, and Callaghan—it acknow-
ledged the burgeoning new talents of the fifties by also including
W.O. Mitchell, Malcolm Lowry, Mordecai Richler, Mavis Gallant,
and Alice Munro.

The English-born writer **Malcolm Lowry** (1909-57)—who lived
in the 1940s at Dollarton, B.C., working on his famous novel *Under
the Volcano* (1947)—produced a small but distinguished group of
lyrical parabolic stories. 'The Bravest Boat', which appears in the
Weaver anthology, is a somewhat pallid evocation of the triumph
of the human spirit over great physical and spiritual torment, a
struggle imaged here by the survival of a frail balsa-wood boat in
the storms and currents of the Pacific. **W.O. Mitchell** (b.1914),
who appears in this anthology with 'The Owl and the Bens', worked
in another tradition—that of the realistic prairie story—varying the
mould of Grove and Ross by adding his own salty humour and
gentle iconoclasm. At the other end of the short-story spectrum,
the stories in *The Street* (1969) by **Mordecai Richler** (b.1931) ex-
tend the urban tradition of Callaghan and Garner into the side-
streets of wartime Montreal's Jewish neighbourhood surrounding
St Urbain St. 'Benny, the War in Europe, and Myerson's Daughter
Bella', despite its paratactic title, is a tightly packed meditation on
the family unit, and on the failure of its solidarity to close the
wounds of wartime service. The simple youth, Benny—unfavourably compared all his life to 'the Shapiro boy'—crumples
under the twin forces of patriarchal ambition and shell-shock. His
suicide is rendered more pathetic by the reader's sense that he almost made it, that family pride (from his brother and mother), and
love (from his wife and new son) could, and almost did, overcome
Benny's great fear of destruction from above.

Among this group of newer writers in the Weaver anthology,
Mavis Gallant ('The Legacy') and Alice Munro ('The Time of

Death') would emerge in the next decade as the foremost Canadian writers of the short story, achieving international as well as national recognition. It is to Weaver's credit that in 1960—when the future strengths and proliferation of the Canadian short story could not have been foreseen—he not only summed up the best of the old but accurately perceived the direction that would be taken in looking ahead to the achievements of Gallant and Munro, which their stories in this collection anticipated.

3

MAVIS GALLANT

In 1950, after working for six years on the Montreal *Standard*, Mavis Gallant (b.1922) settled in Paris, where she still lives. One of her short stories was accepted by *The New Yorker* in 1951, marking the beginning of Gallant's long and distinguished career as a contributor of fiction to its pages. Her *oeuvre* also includes novellas, novels, reviews, and essays, though she is most esteemed internationally as a short-story writer.

Gallant is reticent in print and in interviews about the inspiration, composition, and meaning of her stories, and her narrative voice suggests an unyielding detachment from the characters and situations (one that does not preclude compassion) that is well suited to the kind of subtle satire and humorous effects at which she excels. Her stories exhibit a precise control of language, with sparing use of metaphor, and often focus on exiles and foreigners in Europe or North America who have erected barriers between themselves and an alien environment. Gallant's deft evocation of the language and gesture of such characters highlights the limited nature of the communication that results from such isolation and alienation.

The stories of Mavis Gallant have remained remarkably consistent in subject matter and setting over more than thirty years. Her first collection, *The Other Paris* (1956)—containing stories from 1952 to 1954—presents the four settings that appear in three-quarters of all Gallant's stories: Paris, Quebec, the French Riviera, and Germany. Also evident here is her preoccupation with the rootless foreigner—American, Canadian, or European—stranded in a European setting. Gallant portrays an outsider's vision of the postwar world, as seen through the eyes of exiles, often from a child's point of view. In the social world of these stories isolation, self-delusion, and diminished or non-existent communication abound. Only the endings, where Gallant's final paragraphs soften the dispassionate perspective, identify them with early rather than later work. This gentler tone can be seen in the closing lines of 'About Geneva,' and 'Going Ashore'.

The Other Paris contains stories with a European setting (nine) and a Canadian setting (three). The Quebec stories, here as elsewhere, focus either on the dilemma of the displaced anglophone child ('Wing's Chips') or on the family tensions and conspiracies surrounding an unmarried daughter ('Deceptions of Marie-Blanche', 'The Legacy'). The European stories depict the uneasy exile of Americans ('A Day Like Any Other'), or their occupation of various European locations ('The Picnic,' 'Autumn Day').

These Americans—the Marshall family in 'The Picnic,' and the young soldier Walt and his teenaged bride Cissy in 'Autumn Day'—are part of the postwar American occupation of Europe. Caught between the military hierarchy and power they represent, and the older lines of class, wealth, and culture that still define French and Austrian life, they can do nothing right. Young Cissy is out of place among the wrack of Europeans washed up at Herr Enrich's farmhouse outside Salzburg. In this story, all lines of communication are down: husbands and wives do not talk; letters remain unread or undelivered. Each of the characters longs to confess, and yet the greatest crime is the telling of secrets; all communication between people becomes a possible act of social espionage.

In 'The Picnic' Gallant portrays the clash of cultures between the French townspeople and the Americans at a nearby army post. Major Marshall and his wife are involved in a cold war with their coquettish elderly French landlady, Madame Pégurin, and their children's fascination with her is seen by Mrs Marshall as a threat to their proper upbringing. The Major is in charge of organizing a picnic in the town, planned as an act of rapprochement—'a symbol of unity between two nations'—but even at this festivity the battle lines between cultures remain. In response to a suggestion that

French folk dances be included in the day's activities, the Major is firm: 'Baseball is as far as I'll go.' He must, however, persuade Madame Pégurin, the charming, trivial, and flirtatious old-guard Frenchwoman, that her attendance at the picnic is important symbolically. Madame, who dislikes foreigners, is clever, devious, and manipulative, and tries to outflank the Major at every turn:

> He had convinced Madame Pégurin that she was a symbol only after a prolonged teatime wordplay that bordered on flirtation. This was second nature to Madame Pégurin, but the Major had bogged down quickly. He kept coming around to the point, and Madame Pégurin found the point uninteresting.

The Americans in 'A Day Like Any Other' are part of the economic, not the military, occupation. Exiled from their own country by Mr Kennedy's selfish hypochondria, the family is stranded in Europe. They live from day to day; for both mother and children time is something to be 'passed', as they await the invalid's pleasure—his recovery, removal, or, more remotely, death. Here again, Gallant chooses the plight of the children of exiles to examine the spiritual confusion and restlessness engendered by peripatetic lives.

Children on whom the burden of decoding adult innuendo is seen to fall are again the focus in 'About Geneva'. Whereas, in the reigning social and familial silence of 'A Day Like Any Other,' and 'Autumn Day,' 'telling' is considered dangerous, it becomes an act of power in 'About Geneva'—forbidden to the repressed adults, but still possible to the children, who have not yet been completely socialized according to their divorced mother's and their grandmother's stultifying codes of propriety in life and language.

From the innuendo and body language of the two women in 'About Geneva', Ursula and Colin learn that information can be conveyed without actually being guilty of 'telling' about their visit to their father in Geneva. Ursula raises eyebrows by offering negative comments on his companion's housekeeping, but Colin is too young to understand fully the manoeuvres so well mastered by his sister. Having fed the swans in Geneva is infinitely more important to his child's imagination than his father's domestic life, but he lies to attract attention, saying that he was sick on the plane.

Ironically this fib becomes, for his grandmother, his most satisfactory revelation about Geneva.

> 'Isn't that child in bed yet?' called Granny. 'Does he want his supper?'
> 'No,' said Colin.
> 'No,' said his mother. 'He was sick on the plane.'
> 'I thought so,' Granny said. 'That, at least, is a fact.'

The cryptic communications and misunderstandings in 'About Geneva' stem not only from reticence but also from self-delusion, a human frailty that flourishes among the exiles in the world of Gallant's fiction. For example, Carol, the American girl in 'The Other Paris,' perhaps the best story in the collection, nurtures an illusion of a tantalizingly romantic 'other' version of Paris, just around the corner from the drab, rain-washed Paris streets she inhabits. On the threshold of a loveless marriage to Howard, an American economist, she yearns to unlock the 'secret' of the Paris 'she had read about'. But when confronted with the passion and squalor of an authentic love affair—between her French co-worker Odile and the refugee Felix—she is appalled. At the story's end, Carol muses about her future:

> Soon she sensed the comforting vision of Paris as she had once imagined it would overlap the reality. To have met and married Howard there would sound romantic and interesting, more and more so as time passed. She would forget the rain and her unshared confusion and loneliness, and remember instead the Paris of films, the street lamps with their tinsel icicles, the funny concert hall where the ceiling collapsed, and there would be, at last, a coherent picture, accurate but untrue. The memory of Felix and Odile and all their distasteful strangeness would slip away; for 'love' she would think, once more, 'Paris,' and after a while, happily married, mercifully removed in time, she would remember it and describe it and finally believe it as it had never been at all.

Though this ending is replete with ironies, its tone is one of compassion. Looking out of windows and into possible futures, or romantic pasts, the characters in this early collection see prospects that are less bleak than those offered to their peers in later Gallant stories. Thus the neglected twelve-year-old Emma in 'Going Ashore', unhappy with her nomadic life on a luxury liner with her shallow and flirtatious single mother, cherishes a delusion of safe arrival, of solid ground in a welcoming haven, that is still alive in the closing paragraph of that story:

> Yes, they were nearly there. She could see the gulls swooping and soaring, and something on the horizon—a shape, a rock, a whole continent untouched and unexplored. A tide of newness came in with the salty air; she thought of new land, new dresses, clean, untouched, unworn. A new life. She knelt, patient, holding the curtain, waiting to see the approach to shore.

One of the strengths of the collection, and of all Gallant's stories involving children, is her ability to capture the child's perspective without a trace of condescension. The narrator makes us feel the fascinations, obsessions, and mysteries of a child's life ('Wing's Chips'), but also its terrors ('Going Ashore,' 'A Day Like Any Other').

Also notable in these stories is Gallant's skill in fusing subject and setting. The Riviera stories provide the best illustration of her ability to make the place and the event cohere and interpenetrate. Gallant portrays the lodging houses and hotels of the Riviera stories as a precinct of transients, well suited to her exploration of exile, isolation, and self-delusion. Particularly in later stories such as 'An Unmarried Man's Summer,' the Riviera, which harbours refugees from other epochs, becomes a museum of mores, a fitting place to study the habits and the habitat of dying breeds.

Another characteristic of the stories in this collection—to become a feature of all Gallant's later writing—is the laconic but telling irony that she employs, seemingly without national bias. She can transform a simple detail, such as the food eaten by her characters, into an exposé of their personalities. Here she reveals the essence of Paula Marshall, the vapid American wife in 'The Picnic':

> Paula was suspicious of extravagant tastes or pleasures. She enjoyed the nursery food she gave the children, sharing without question their peas and lamb chops, their bland and innocent desserts. Once, long ago, she had broken off an engagement only because she had detected in the young man's eyes a look of sensuous bliss as he ate strawberries and cream. And now her own children came to the table full of rum-soaked sponge cake and looked with condescension at their lemon jello.

If there is any defect in these stories, it lies in the not-yet-perfected narrative voice. In four of them Gallant uses a first-person narrator instead of the detached third-person commentator that would eventually become her hallmark. In 'Wing's Chips' the first-person retrospective successfully recreates the experience of the little girl whose artist father defies convention by living among French Canadians and refusing to join the paid labour force, preferring instead to practise his art. The father, however, does paint a sign for the fish-and-chip shop belonging to the Wing family, and though the commission results from a misunderstanding of the word 'painter', and no money ever changes hands, the daughter is proud of this 'proof' that her father is finally 'an ordinary workingman just like anybody else'. In some other stories, however, such as 'The Deceptions of Marie-Blanche,' 'Autumn Day', and 'Senor Pinedo,' the first-person narrative is less deftly handled. The 'I' in 'Deceptions' is a family figure completely peripheral to the main courtship action; and in 'Senor Pinedo' an even more faceless 'I' hovers in the corner of the story. In later collections Gallant would phase out the peripheral I-observer, although often retaining the retrospective 'I' for stories of childhood (for example, 'The Wedding Ring', 1969).

Her next collection, *My Heart is Broken* (1964), differs from its predecessor in containing a 'short novel', 'Its Image on the Mirror.' Eight stories make up the rest of the volume, including two from Quebec ('Bernadette' and the title story), and three Riviera stories, two of which are among the best Gallant ever wrote: 'Acceptance of Their Ways', and 'An Unmarried Man's Summer'.

In these two stories Gallant continues her examination of the truncated lives of people displaced to the Riviera, a backwater where, even in the 1950s, a semblance of the secure pre-war lifestyle can be maintained. The three gentlewomen (one is the impostor Lily Littel) in 'Acceptance of Their Ways' (1960) are shown living a circumscribed life on this 'quiet shore', and indulging in the only pastime feasible in their isolation, that of excoriating each other. The seemingly mild domestic setting of the lodging house emerges under Gallant's scrutiny as a battleground where words and food are the main weapons. But Lily, who 'looked soft', but who 'could have bitten a real pearl in two and enjoyed the pieces', dissembles in order to get on:

> If Lily had settled for this bleached existence, it was explained by a sentence scrawled over a page of her locked diary: 'I live with gentlewomen now.' And there was a finality about the statement that implied acceptance of their ways.

The other Riviera story, 'An Unmarried Man's Summer' (1963), introduces another dominant theme in Gallant's fiction—the effect of the Second World War on Europe and its inhabitants. Walter, the English bachelor of the title, horribly burned in the war, has retreated to a villa where he ekes out an existence with a meagre pension, and amuses himself by playing gigolo to ageing British and American widows, while awaiting eviction from the house on the inevitable return of its owners.

Gallant uses a clever metaphor of the mosaic to portray the kind of order Walter imposes on his transient way of life:

> A mosaic picture of Walter's life early in the summer of his forty-fifth year would have shown him dead center, where nothing can seem more upsetting than a punctured tire or more thrilling than a sunny day.

In the elegantly crafted mosaic of his life, Walter has included his two servants—Angelo, the teen-aged illegal immigrant, and Mme Rossi, the *femme de ménage* : 'The figures make a balanced and nearly perfect design supported by a frieze of pallida iris. . . .' But this 'perfect design' is disrupted by the summer visit of Walter's sister and her family, who invade the quiet villa with the tug-of-war of middle-class family life. On their departure, both Walter and Angelo are upset—Walter by a yearning, hitherto unsuspected, for the affection and esteem of his niece, and Angelo by a longing for family life and a promise of the wider world. As Walter prepares to transform the events of the summer into a witty tale for the entertainment of the widows, the reader understands that all of Walter's life is story material—a fictitious mosaic that comes to life only in the embroidered retelling where Walter's fabrications transform the empty reality. Their mode of existence is cruel to Angelo, and stultifying for Walter; but both, pathetically, remain frozen into the false harmony of the mosaic design.

It is typical of Gallant's approach that the story should end not with pathos but with irony. The detached tone of her narrative voice allows no sentimental illusions to flourish in the mind of the reader. This story also features—as do many others—an evocation of the Second World War as a line of demarcation between an idyllic past and a turbulent present. 'An Unmarried Man's Summer' is one of the earliest Gallant stories in which she makes palpable the weight of the war and its accompanying history that presses down on the characters. There are scars not only on Walter's body, but on his premises: 'Walter has a faded old *Viva* on the door to his garage,' a 'relic of the Italian occupation of the coast.'

A precursor of Angelo appears in the earlier story 'Bernadette' (1957), which, though set in Montreal, offers a similar picture of a master-servant relationship. The young French Canadian, Bernadette, is baffled by the liberal attitudes of her employers and drifts passively into a pregnancy that may shatter the household.

A much stronger, though shorter, story is 'My Heart is Broken', set in a mining camp in the north woods of Quebec. Jeannie, like Bernadette, is a figure of curiously tainted innocence; her ignorance stems from a refusal to know. The central riddle of the story—who assaulted Jeannie, if anyone, and why?—is never cleared up. Gallant's spare dialogue suggests hidden depths of meaning, but offers few facts.

Much of the haunting power of this story emanates from the enigma, from the silences that loom larger than the spoken word. This pared-down technique is also used in one of the Paris stories in this volume, 'Sunday Afternoon', whose dialogue—reminiscent of Hemingway's—reveals the hidden tensions among three people in a small apartment, by hinting at the ripple of sex, sexism, and politics beneath the scattering of words on the surface.

In the early seventies, McClelland and Stewart decided to include a selection of Gallant's stories in their New Canadian Library series, and *The End of the World and Other Stories*, edited by Robert Weaver, was published in 1974. It included three stories from each of the two previous collections, and seven that had been published in *The New Yorker* between 1967 and 1971.

The End of the World includes a group of Gallant's shortest stories. 'The Wedding Ring' (1969), at 1,500 words, is the shortest and the best of three first-person narratives that include 'The End of the World' (1967), and 'The Prodigal Parent' (1969). All three present a world of pain and dislocation that follows a child's estrangement from a parent. In 'The Wedding Ring' the terrible hurt of the daughter is cast into relief by the almost lyrical quality of the imagery and description. The concrete images crisply set out at the opening of the story convey both the clarity and the fragmentation of childhood memories:

> On my windowsill is a pack of cards, a bell, a dog's brush, a book about a girl named Jewel who is a Christian scientist and won't let anyone take her temperature,...and a white jug holding field flowers. The water in the jug has evaporated; the sand-and-amber flowers seem made of paper.

In this dry, papery world, the little girl craves love and recognition from her fey, vixenish mother, and finds it in one brief summer day when they wash their hair together in a stream. For the child it is a baptism of happiness and unity. The memory of that one moment of identification with her mother seems to transcend a history of separation and longing, and gives her, as retrospective adult narrator, a means of understanding her mother's action in casting off her wedding ring. Entering imaginatively into the act, the grown-up daughter pictures its resting place:

> First it slipped under one of those sharp bluish stones, then a beetle moved it. It left its print on a cushion of moss after the first winter.

In a final act of reconciliation and forgiveness, she acknowledges, and even seems to cherish, an intangible inheritance from her mother:

> No one else could have worn it. My mother's hands were small, like mine.

All the stories in *The Pegnitz Junction: A Novella and Five Short Stories* (1973) are about Germans, and were written out of a need to understand the sources of fascism, 'its small possibilities in people'. In 1977 Gallant said: 'This is the favourite of my books; the title story, the novella, is the favourite of all my writing.' In this novella an unmarried German couple and a little boy—Christine, Herbert, and his son—leave Paris after a week's holiday and travel by train, arriving after many delays at Pegnitz, the junction where they change trains for the homeward journey. Through Christine we enter the heads of other passengers, and of people seen or met at stations. Their utterances, their thoughts, and the actions that mask their thoughts, are skilfully interwoven in this collage of lifelike, ordinary Germans. The collection is unified by its alternating focus—between the characters in the foreground and a background of history—theirs, the country's, and Europe's. In 'The Old Friends,' for example, a simple, pleasant ritual encounter between a respectable Commissioner and the ageing actress he sporadically courts, is played out against a tense backdrop of the holocaust and its impact on both their past lives. As in so many of Gallant's later stories, the characters' pasts are embedded in their being. The German Police Commissioner, an ordinary man, still feels the weight of guilt when Helena alludes to her Jewish origins. A survivor of transit camps, she seems to have outlived her hell, to have returned, impossibly, to a vacated Eden, the hotel garden where she sips champagne with the Commissioner. But the very tension between foreground and background signals that the innocence and *bonhomie* of the present-day Eden is both carefully crafted and tenuously maintained.

'Ernst in Civilian Clothes', a cryptic story, spare in style and emotion, also dwells on the war's legacy of displacement—both geographical and psychic—as it charts a day in the life of the ex-Legionnaire, returning to a German 'homeland' that was not his birthplace. Having expediently lost and gained national identity several times in his young life, Ernst no longer possesses a sense of what the truth is, personally or historically: 'Everyone is lying; he will invent his own truth. Is it important if one-tenth of a lie is true?'

Ernst is sunk in a delusion much more dangerous than that of Carol in the early story 'The Other Paris'. In her case, the delusion of a romantic Paris and of her own participation in it is a personal one, pathetic but forgivable. The stories of *The Pegnitz Junction*, however, are pervaded with delusions about the separation between wartime values and the realities of the present that emerge as damaging perversions of the truth.

It was not until the publication in Toronto of Gallant's *From the Fifteenth District* (1979) that her writing began to receive prominent attention in Canada. This collection—the title refers to the fifteenth *arrondissement* of Paris—returns to one of Gallant's favourite territories in three of her best Riviera stories: 'The Four Seasons' (1975), 'The Moslem Wife' (1976), and 'The Remission' (1979). All three chronicle the impact of the war on a woman. Barbara, Carmela, and Netta, though very different, are consummate survivors. As the world crumbles around them, they change and adapt, mutating into a species suited to the new world created by war and its aftermath. The metaphor of mutation, best developed in 'The Remission', articulates the downfall of one kind of pre-war European male—Alec—and the rise of a younger, more adaptable species, personified in the opportunist Eric. Between them sits Alec's wife Barbara, whose eventual reversal of loyalties is perhaps the most spectacular mutation of all. Barbara installs her lover, the brash Eric, in her household, even as Alec is dying slowly in the nearby French hospital. In the memories of her children, this unceremonious changing of the guard signals the end of an Edenic childhood existence and their initiation into a harsher world where they will be perpetual exiles and expatriates.

'The Four Seasons', a story about the thirteen-year-old Italian peasant Carmela, portrays one small life battered by the shifting tides of world events; it ranks with the best of Gallant's evocations of a child's view of the world. Carmela's naïve, yet instinctively shrewd, outlook exposes the insular, caste-ridden expatriate English society of pre-war Liguria. Here Gallant has perfected the controlled distancing of her narrative tone, which allows sympathy with Carmela and understanding of her plight, but prevents sentimental illusions about her. Abandoned by the retreating English family, Carmela does what she can to ensure survival. Her request for wages is rejected by Mrs Unwin: 'But Carmela, you seemed so fond of the children!' Denied money, Carmela decides to take at least what food she needs for her long journey home:

The larder was still unlocked. She took a loaf of bread and cut it in three pieces and hid the pieces in her case. Many years later, it came to her that in lieu of wages she should have taken a stone [a precious stone] from the leather box. Only fear would have kept her from doing it, if she had thought of it.

Carmela is treated as a thief when she leaves; her employers seem unaware that the bread amounts to a mere token of what is owed to the girl who has been raising their children:

When Mrs. Unwin searched Carmela's case—Carmela expected that; everyone did it with servants—she found the bread, looked at it without understanding, and closed the lid. Carmela waited to be told more.

The distilled omniscience of Gallant's narrator, which seeps through in the observation, 'Many years later, it came to her . . .', is a device used in several stories in this volume (for example in 'Potter' and 'The Remission'). This technique increases the perspectives on the events narrated, and implies that in the end all truths are relative truths.

In 'Potter', a very long story, the truths narrated are those of the sporadic love affair between Piotr, a Polish intellectual, and Laurie, a young Canadian vagabond, who lives a free life as house-sitter, beggar, and mistress in Europe. Potter (Laurie's uneducated western pronunciation of 'Piotr') is fascinated with the freedom that Laurie embodies; to him, shackled to the past, to his country's history, to visas, permits, and passports, Laurie is almost dangerously unfettered, ignorant of her own shallow history, and serenely unmindful of national boundaries as she drifts from lover to lover. The narrator of 'Potter' is a third-person voice of limited omniscience and extreme urbanity that conveys all of Piotr's thoughts and motivations, his past and his future, but deals with Laurie only in terms of what is known to Piotr, to whom the western Laurie is inscrutable. In this story Gallant refines the 'Many years later' technique used in 'The Four Seasons' by making the narrator allied to Piotr, but not identical with him; nor is the narrator Piotr-in-the-future, but perhaps Piotr distilled, rarefied, and freed from the constraints of time. Gallant often uses phrases like 'In his later memories . . .' to draw attention to Piotr's recollection of events surrounding the love affair, and to suggest his future reconstruction of them. This technique subtly implies that the selection of events presented forms only one version of the story. Truth, from this narrative perspective, is a relative thing; the past for such Gallant narrators contains only a selection of possible stories, each of which is simply one re-creation of plausible truths.

Another narrative trait first exhibited in *From the Fifteenth District* is the flattened documentary tone of the brief title story, which reports an 'epidemic of hauntings' in this Parisian district and concentrates on three particular case studies. Borrowing the factual third-person style (and some of the jargon) of courtroom journalism, Gallant successfully inverts stereotypes by presenting absurdities in a logical, cut-and-dried manner: 'Mrs. Carlotte Essling, née Holmquist, complains of being haunted by her husband, Professor Augustus Essling, the philosopher and historian.' The haunting is treated as a civic nuisance. Mrs Essling 'suggests that the police find some method of keeping him [her husband's ghost] off the streets. The police ought to threaten him; frighten him; put the fear of the Devil into him.'

This ironic account of a fairly conventional haunting is the last in a trio of case studies that begins with an inverted haunting: a ghost is haunted by the congregation of the church he visits once a year on the anniversary of his own death. The ghost complains that all the superstitious nonsense engendered by his annual visit is an invasion of his privacy. Between these two 'ghost stories', and also occurring in the Fifteenth District of Paris, is a domestic tragedy of poverty and disease, whose distressing end is conveyed in the metaphorical haunting of the dead immigrant, Mrs Ibrahim, by doctors and social workers, belatedly anatomizing her 'case.' The account, peppered with bureaucratic jargon—'ratification and approval,' 'social investigator,' 'relinquished her right to a domicile'—resembles a deposition given to the police, and the careful taking of evidence in the interest of seeing justice done. Mrs Ibrahim, deceased mother of twelve children, 'asks that her account of the afternoon [of her death] be registered with the police as the true version and that copies be sent to the Doctor and the social investigator, with a courteous request for peace and silence'.

Nothing like justice is done in any of these 'cases', although the complainant pleads to some invisible court for peace, privacy, dignity, and the right to die (or live) without public outcry and outrage. Underlying the stories is Gallant's satire on the failure of bureaucracy, and the paradoxical reliance on its methods even by its victim. Gallant would return to this ironic documentary style in several recent satirical stories, including 'Leaving the Party' (uncollected), and 'The Assembly' (*Overhead in a Balloon*).

Home Truths (1981) is a collection of stories, some of them early, with Canadian characters and settings. With its feisty title and Canadian content, this volume might well have been groomed for approval by the Canadian literary establishment (it won a Governor General's Award). It is divided into three sections, the first of which, entitled 'At Home', contains stories with exclusively Canadian settings. Some of these are among Gallant's earliest stories: 'Thank You For the Lovely Tea (1956), 'Jorinda and Jorindel' (1959), and 'Up North' (1959). The second section, 'Canadians Abroad', reprints two of her best studies of exile, 'In the Tunnel' (1971) and 'The Ice Wagon Going Down the Street' (1963), and also includes two less interesting stories, 'Bonaventure' (1966) and 'Virus X' (1965).

Of these, 'The Ice Wagon Going Down the Street' is the most frequently anthologized. It is a study of two exiled Canadians, the irresponsible social climber, Peter Frazier, and the earnest prairie girl, Agnes Brusen. Peter has drifted to Geneva in search of an undemanding job that will enable him to maintain his tenuous links with the world of diplomats and socialites. He meets Agnes when they are assigned to the same office in some unnamed and presumably functionless 'agency'. Although both are Canadians, Agnes and Peter are polar opposites, from two different worlds—that of the Norwegian immigrant in Saskatchewan, and that of an upper-class Ontario dynasty. In the aftermath of a disastrous costume party, Agnes and Peter share a moment of awkward communion, in which Agnes offers her most treasured memory of solitude and isolation:

> I've never been alone before. When I was a kid I would get up in the summer before the others, and I'd see the ice wagon going down the street. . . . That was the best. It's the best you can hope to have. In a big family, if you want to be alone, you have to get up before the rest of them. You get up early in the morning in the summer and it's you, you, once in your life alone in the universe. You think you know everything that can happen. . . . Nothing is ever like that again.

Though his social instincts rebel against it, Peter is touched by the confidence, and even feels drawn to Agnes by the revelation that she shares his sense of solitude, and of living in a world fallen away from an early and impossible ideal. Although 'nothing happened' between them, Agnes becomes 'the only secret Peter has from his wife'. The tawdry but glamorous Sheilah would never understand what they shared: 'They were both Canadians, so they had this much together—the knowledge of the little you dare admit.' Gallant's ice-wagon, though appearing so fleetingly in the story, haunts its pages, and becomes an austere but evocative symbol of the solace of solitude at the core of the human heart.

The third and final section of *Home Truths*, 'Linnet Muir', contains a group of six stories, each dealing with the life of an intelligent young woman in Montreal. It is to these stories that readers and critics look for the autobiographical material that Gallant so continually denies her public. Linnet breaks free from her family and 'the prison of her childhood' and finds in wartime Montreal 'the natural background of [her] exile and fidelity.' The resemblance to Gallant herself becomes persuasive when Linnet—a name that, like 'Mavis', is the name of a songbird—reveals herself as a writer: 'Anything I could not decipher I turned into fiction, which was my way of untangling knots' ('Varieties of Exile'). This gathering of six stories includes four from this period of personal revolution in wartime dislocation, and two from Linnet's childhood—'Voices Lost in the Snow', and 'The Doctor'. The final piece in the group, 'With a Capital T', differs in tone from the others, the satire being gentler and lighter. Humour is paramount in this story, particularly in the opening pages, as Linnet recounts her struggle to find 'Truth with a capital T' in her job as a writer of captions for newspaper photographs.

Two clusters of stories dominate *Overhead in a Balloon* (1985): a group of three dealing with petty jealousy and infighting in the European literary community ('A Painful Affair', 'A Flying Start', and 'Grippes and Poche') and four retrospective first-person narratives centring on the elusive Magdalena ('A Recollection', 'Rue de Lille', 'The Colonel's Child', and 'Lena').

The title story, however, belongs to a third group, and thus offers a misleadingly bouncy title for what is an austere volume, in which the humour is strictly literary. 'Overhead in a Balloon' is linked thematically with 'Speck's Idea', the story of almost novella length that opens the collection. Both stories explore the byways of the Parisian art world; not the glamour of the larger galleries and the Old Masters, but the decayed gentility of the small side-street galleries where minor works and trends are lionized. In 'Speck's Idea' the owner of such a gallery campaigns for an exhibition that will make a name for himself and for the gallery. Sandor Speck's discreet battle with an artist's widow is played out against a background of city terrorism—a constant threat of death and anarchy that, like the gallery itself, has its roots in the past. Both conflicts in this story, the artistic and the political, are merely surface skirmishes in a much older and deeper war between the forces of civilization and those of anarchy. The companion story, 'Overhead in a Balloon', involves a tactical war over living accommodation and again features the plight of the outsider. Contained in the balloon metaphor is a sense of the outsider set adrift in a foreign element where behaviour and language are over his head. Walter—the Swiss gallery-assistant in 'Speck's Idea'—risks a 'long, dangerous trapeze swoop of friendship' with a French artist and moves in with him and his relations; 'for the first time since he had left Bern to work in Paris, he felt close to France.' But the friendship fails to develop, the French family becomes increasingly enigmatic to him—what is said to him 'is clear, but a kind of secret'—and he senses that 'one of these days he was going to lose momentum and be left dangling without a safety net'. While Walter vacations with his family in Bern, where there are 'no secrets, no mysteries', the owner of the house (a weekend balloonist) sits in Walter's apartment, planning his eviction; the plastic dust-sheets Walter had spread over his furniture lie 'like crumpled parachutes in a corner'.

The crucial question of accommodation in a crowded Parisian world recurs in the stories that deal with the rivalry between the French man of letters, Henri Grippes, and the English writer, Victor Prism. Gallant's depiction of the battles between these two old literary war-horses produces an effect of dry hilarity—the result of a series of cumulative satiric thrusts. In 'A Painful Affair' Grippes and Prism conduct a pointed and none-too-genteel scuffle over the rights to enjoy the patronage and memory of a deceased literary benefactor: Mary Margaret Pugh, who 'did not believe in art, only in artists.' A similar atmosphere of literary jostling pervades the second story in the Grippes cluster, 'A Flying Start'. Here Gallant lampoons the creaking machinery of the French literary establishment, its espousal of ponderous Herculean labours, in this case the editing of a massive volume to be titled *Living Authors of the Fourth Republic*. Inevitably the writing of the work takes so long that the title and contents begin to date. Some of the 'living' authors presumably vacate the category, and the Fourth Republic slides into the Fifth long before Grippes and his ilk have made their contributions to its pages. One working title of this project, *Contemporary Writers, Women and Others*, reveals Gallant's satirical view of the sectarianism and narrow-mindedness of the French literary establishment. In the third and final Grippes story, 'Grippes and Poche', the incorrigible writer takes on not the literati but the bureaucracy. Grippes engages in a life-long struggle with O. Poche, a civil servant with the Income Tax Department who audits Grippes' irregular tax file. The relations between Grippes and Poche, however, involve more than a struggle over Grippes' income; the plundering is distinctly mutual. Grippes uses Poche as the model for a string of middle-class male characters in a series of well-received novels. In this story the parasitic relationship between art and life stands revealed as a kind of sordid symbiosis, which characterizes not only these three Grippes stories, but also 'Speck's Idea' and 'Overhead in a Balloon'.

In a different vein are the stories from the second cluster—the Magdalena stories—which form a solid block of four towards the end of the volume. These hark back technically to some of Gallant's earliest stories, using a first-person narrator with a retrospective point of view. Gallant's short stories had shown a movement *away* from the first person (which was awkwardly employed in some stories from *The Other Paris*), and *towards* a distilled third-person point of view, such as that employed in the Grippes stories. But in the Magdalena group the first-person narrator, Magdalena's husband, chronicles his past and that of his two wives in interlocking narrative loops that circle through the four stories. Throughout, Lena plays the part of the alluring, unattainable woman, to whom the narrator was technically married, but whom he has never possessed in any sense of the word. In 'A Recollection', the Jewish Magdalena escapes with her young husband from the advancing Germans, fleeing into a glamorous shadow-world of survival and obscurity, from which she later emerges to plague the narrator's second wife, Juliette ('Rue de Lille', 'The Colonel's Child'). The image of Juliette, seen knitting at the end of 'Rue de Lille', captures her relation to the perversely surviving Lena: 'She was knitting squares of wool to be sewn together to make a blanket; there was always somewhere a flood or an earthquake or a flow of refugees, and those who outlasted jeopardy had to be covered.' As one who has 'outlasted jeopardy', Lena is reminiscent of the ageing actress of an earlier story, 'The Old Friends'; both women conceal uncomfortable historical and racial memories under a façade of charm. In the final story of the group, 'Lena', the title character is 'eighty and bedridden' but still indomitable, having outlived the narrator's second, and younger, wife. With an improbable tenacity, Lena assumes a place in the narrator's life, not just in his past, but also at the centre of his present life. Even her hospital bed is occupied territory: 'Magdalena cannot be evicted—not just like that. She has no family, and nowhere to go.' The relationship between the narrator and Lena presents a dilemma common in Mavis Gallant's fiction—the impossibility of 'evicting' the uncomfortable elements of the past to create a comfortable and convenient present.

The strengths and concerns of *Overhead in a Balloon* are virtually identical with those of Gallant's earliest collections. Some of the realism and incipient sentiment of early stories have given way to a more stylized treatment, and the tone is more detached, placing greater emphasis on collective wrongs rather than on individual foibles. But Gallant's overriding interest in the sub-text of daily life—the messages in the unspoken word, the hidden gesture—is still evident in a late story such as 'Speck's Idea'. Over three decades Gallant's fiction has moved through the same fictional territory—mainly post-war Europe, but also the Montreal and environs of her early years—poking at the surface appearances of the world, exposing underlying truths, few of them pleasant. On the one hand, hers is a fiction of social and political satire, exposing the hypocrisy of institutionalized reconstructions of history. On another level her work also reveals that much hypocrisy inevitably stems from individual psychology; the personal and the particular are always present in Gallant's fiction, even in the most stylized of the late stories. With their multi-layered European sensibility, Gallant's stories have a more sophisticated appeal than do those of her contemporaries and successors in the Canadian short story. And the distilled omniscience of her characteristic narrator—whose voice speaks from an elevated plane, with knowledge of the past and insight into the future—has marked out a fictional territory that Gallant owns.

4

ALICE MUNRO

Alice Munro's first short-story collection, *Dance of the Happy Shades*, won a Governor General's Award for fiction in 1968, only five years after Hugh Garner's collection had won the same award. That the short story could twice within several years beat out heavy competition from the novel was an indication of the genre's new resurgence and popularity in the sixties. Garner himself wrote the foreword to *Dance of the Happy Shades*, and in some ways Munro's early stories belonged in the Garner tradition—a fiction of the ordinary person, written in ordinary language. Munro has since produced four more collections of her stories of small-town life in Southwestern Ontario: *Something I've Been Meaning to Tell You* (1974), *Who Do You Think You Are?* (1978), *The Moons of Jupiter* (1982), and *The Progress of Love* (1986).

Her first collection, however, was notable for several stories whose technical complexity indicated that she was already moving far beyond the well-made magazine story that Garner wrote so skilfully. His form owed a debt to the rigorously structured O. Henry story of the early twentieth century. In the typical Garner story action is one-dimensional and unified; the story has a 'point' and moves relentlessly towards it. But the structure in much of Munro's fiction (and increasingly in her later stories) is spatial rather than linear. As she has said, she sees the story not as a 'road, taking me somewhere', but more as a 'house' for the reader to move around in and to 'stay in' for a while.

Inside the houses of Munro's fiction the reader sometimes meets a narrator who is neither detached nor objective, whose involvement in the events being related forces the reader to play detective, to comb the text for clues to the 'full story' behind the selected revelations of the narration. The narrators also tend to call attention to the literary form of their own material, raising questions about the relation of life to art and, as in the story 'Material' from *Something I've Been Meaning to Tell You*, examining the technical process and the ethical implications of transforming 'material' from ordinary lives into artistic material. Dotty, the 'harlot-in-residence' in this story, lives in a basement apartment in a 'downtown boardinghouse for men' run by her mother:

> Her rooms were full of heavy furniture salvaged from her marriage—an upright piano, overstuffed chesterfield and chairs, walnut veneer china cabinet and dining room table, where we sat. In the middle of the table was a tremendous lamp with a painted china base and a pleated, dark red silk shade, held out at an extravagant angle, like a hoop skirt.

The narrator, who calls the lamp 'a whorehouse lamp', wants to be congratulated on this characterization by her writer husband: 'I told Hugo he ought to pay more attention to Dotty if he wanted to be a writer.' The conscious literariness in some of these stories can be seen as metafiction, keeping pace with the development of the short story in Europe, Latin America, and North America. But Munro showed a tendency early in her career to use objects, documents, and particularly photographs to gain access to the pasts of her characters in unusual ways, and to create multiple perspectives on family events.

In *Dance of the Happy Shades* experiences and events are told from many points of view—those of childhood, adolescence, and adulthood—and the stories deal with problems of communication between generations or between the sexes. Several treat sex-role stereotyping, as adolescent girls in particular discover the limitations of the roles society has assigned to them ('Boys and Girls', 'Red Dress').

Some of these stories feature revelatory moments reminiscent of the Joycean epiphany, but Munro transforms them into a process of uncovering buried awareness not only in the character but in the reader. In 'Images' the child undergoes a terrifying, but confirming, experience:

People say they have been paralyzed by fear, but I was transfixed, as if struck by lightning, and what hit me did not feel like fear so much as recognition. I was not surprised. This is the sight that does not surprise you, the thing you have always known was there and comes so naturally, moving delicately and contentedly and in no hurry, as if it was made, in the first place, from a wish of yours, a hope of something final, terrifying.

Such moments in Munro's fiction elicit from the reader a flash of recognition as well—their authenticity is verified by a sudden awareness that we have experienced something similar and responded in a like manner. Indeed, this ability to evoke in the reader responses kindred to those of fictional characters whose situations may be vastly different from our own is evident in all Munro's stories; it derives partly from her concern with feelings and with what she calls the 'quality' of people's lives that she wishes to capture in her writing. 'What happens as event doesn't really much matter,' she has said. 'When the event becomes the thing that matters, the story isn't working too well. There has to be a feeling in the story.'

One of the methods of creating this 'feeling' is the loving attention to detail that Munro lavishes on the setting for a situation or event. Very often these details resonate in the mind of the first-person narrator, who draws the reader into the atmosphere or 'quality' of the scene more intimately than might be possible with a third-person narration. About her approach to the arrangement of these settings Munro has said: 'The way people live. The way houses are furnished and all the objects in them. I am crazy about doing this. . . . I like people's clothes, too. I like doing that. I do a lot on surface things.' In 'Thanks for the Ride', an early story first published in 1957 in *The Tamarack Review* (No.2, Winter), we see Lois, the small-town girl who is picked up by two young men on the lookout for an evening's fun, inviting them into her house to wait while she changes her clothes. The narrator—the young man who is to be her 'date'—describes the scene:

The little front room had linoleum on the floor and flowered paper curtains at the windows. There was a glossy chesterfield with a Niagara Falls and a To Mother cushion on it, and there was a little black stove with a screen around it for summer, and a big vase of paper apple blossoms. A tall, frail woman came into the room drying her hands on a dishtowel, which she flung into a chair. Her mouth was full of blue-white china teeth, the long cords trembled in her neck.

After chatting briefly with the woman—Lois's mother—the narrator describes the smell of the place and the mother's voice and extracts from the atmosphere a sense of the 'quality' Munro seeks to convey: 'The smell, the slovenly, confiding voice—something about this life I had not known, something about these people.' The 'something' he senses is the difference between the 'innocence' of his own background and the 'sly and sad' knowingness of Lois's.

The most distinctive feature of Munro's stories is the leisurely, digressive unfolding of the narrative. In its simplest form this non-linear structure involves a diversion of the reader's interest. Munro will engage the reader's attention with one set of circumstances and turn to another, seemingly peripheral, set of events or characters for the dénouement, as in 'How I Met My Husband'. The adolescent housemaid Edie becomes infatuated with an older itinerant pilot, and after his departure spends months waiting for an expected letter to appear in her employer's mailbox. The reader, primed by the title, waits for a romantic fulfilment to be embodied in that letter. In the last few paragraphs we learn that Edie becomes acquainted with the postman while waiting at the mailbox, and that she eventually realizes that *'No letter was ever going to come'* and that she 'was not made' to be the sort of woman who waits 'year after year' for something that may never happen. Nevertheless we are surprised to learn in the final paragraph that she married the postman and settled down to a happy domestic life. Despite this 'twist', the effect of the story does not depend on 'what happens' but on the experience that led to it. Edie's story reveals the depth of romantic yearning that may underlie mundane lives—a yearning that in some sense we share, since otherwise we would not be surprised by the 'twist'.

Munro's digressive narrative strategies become more complex in her later stories, leaving the relatively simple structure of 'How I Met My Husband' far behind. Her latest collections, *The Moons of Jupiter* and *The Progress of Love*, demonstrate that narrative digression and progression are one and the same. 'White Dump', from *The Progress of Love*, epitomizes Munro's meandering narrative technique at its most refined. Here the approaches to the 'quality' of the story are at least three-fold, corresponding roughly to the three-part division of the narrative. Each section presents the viewpoint of a different female figure—Denise, her grandmother Sophie, and Denise's mother Isabel. Despite this apparent focus on the three generations of women, our attention is deflected sideways to the male figure, Denise's father Laurence, who emerges as the central enigma in the story. In the first section Laurence appears as his daughter sees him in the present—remarried, irritatingly conservative—and as she remembers him in the past, on his fortieth birthday, for which young Denise had prepared a special treat: a flight in a small plane. On this outing Isabel initiates an affair with the bold, husky pilot of the plane, a fact that is not revealed until the third section of the story, from Isabel's point of view. Between Denise's section and the completion of the story is Sophie's section, where the ferociously iconoclastic and scholarly grandmother is interrupted in her morning swim by a trio of long-haired 'hippies' who take her bathrobe and cigarettes. This outrage occurs on the same fateful birthday, but the account is not complete until section three, when we learn of the family's reaction to Sophie's arrival, irate and buck-naked, for the celebratory breakfast.

The discontinuous narrative accords with Munro's vision of people 'living in flashes', and her concern with capturing events from different individual perspectives. Thus Sophie's nudity, forced upon her by the theft of her bathrobe, is not something to 'cover up' but merely the culmination of a long series of changes and invasions of her world; to Isabel it is more calculated than careless, a means of making her son Laurence look foolish. Laurence sees his mother's nudity as an embarrassment, a public display of her independence from social convention, a position she has maintained ever since proudly giving birth to Laurence out of wedlock forty years ago. To young Denise it is a pivotal revelation of the effects of age on the female body. Each response bears indirectly on the aftermath of the betrayal that will take place later in the day.

Isabel's adultery will set her free from the prison of conventional family happiness in which Laurence is contentedly caged. Denise will leave other illusions of childhood behind her. And, high up in the plane, Sophie achieves a wider angle of vision on the world.

The ultimate deflection in the story concerns its title. The 'white dump', the castoff icing and marshmallow from a biscuit factory, is described by Isabel as a childhood dream:

> It was something about the White Dump—that there was so much and it was so white and shiny. It was like a kid's dream—the most wonderful promising thing you could ever see.

It does not enter the story until the final section, when Isabel recalls her lower-class childhood, just prior to her taking of the opportunity before her—the offered blond-white body of the pilot and the chance for freedom he stands for. The image of the white dump, like Sophie's nudity earlier in the day, produces different reactions in the family. Isabel's description of the white dump conveys a sense of almost magical bounty waiting to be seized, irresistibly shiny and attractive, like the three wishes offered Laurence for his birthday. The practical Sophie, on the other hand, deplores the unhealthy aspect of the white dump. Denise adopts a sociological stance to explain the mysterious attraction of the dirty sweets: 'That was all they had. They were poor children.' But Laurence's reaction is the most interesting. Because he still cultivates the 'challenge' of Isabel's irrisistible glamour by refusing to let her cut her dark-red hair and by supervising her tan—he had fallen instantly in love with the 'tarty looks' of this 'poor, bright girl from the factory side of town, wearing a tight pink sweater that Laurence always remembered'—his quietly ironic appreciation suggests an affinity with her remembered response to the tawdry appeal of the white dump. The 'pleasure and irony' of his reaction convey an acceptance of Isabel that seems to imply tacit consent for her adulterous adventure.

In contrast to the wandering narrative shape of many of Munro's stories is the variation on the 'twist-at-the-end' in 'Hard-Luck Stories' (*The Moons of Jupiter*). The narrator's ex-lover, Douglas, is having an affair with her friend Julie, a development arising from what seemed a casual introduction two months earlier when all three travelled home together from a conference. To Julie the meeting and the falling in love are 'like one of those ironical-twist-at-the-end sort of stories that used to be so popular'. 'Wouldn't it make a good story?' she asks; 'Why did those stories go out of style?' The narrator, who is just learning about Julie and Douglas now, over lunch with Julie, replies, 'They got to seem too predictable. . . . Or people thought, that isn't the way things happen. Or they thought, who cares the way things happen?'

By airing the notion of the twist ending on the opening page of the story, Munro alerts us to a pattern that will be both fulfilled and subverted. In the conventional twist story, the ironic shift in the plot is the whole point of the story. In 'Hard-Luck Stories', however, the point lies not in the twist given away at the outset, but beyond the plot events—in the situational irony of the story-within-the-story, told by the narrator on the trip home from the conference. Ostensibly contributing her own 'hard-luck story' to the group, she sends a silent message to Douglas that contains a meditation on two kinds of love:

> There's the intelligent sort of love that makes an intelligent choice. That's the kind you're supposed to get married on. Then there's the kind that's anything but intelligent, that's like a possession. And that's the one, that's the one, everybody really values. That's the one nobody wants to have missed out on.

Embedded in all three stories of narrative diversion—'How I Met My Husband', 'White Dump', and 'Hard-Luck Stories'—is a similar notion of the dual nature of love. The form of each story seems to imitate the feelings of the character, feelings that veer from the approved, intelligent course of love and marriage, towards the romance of the imperfect, illicit love affair. Readers acquire sophistication, Munro says; lovers do not. Julie of 'Hard-Luck Stories' sees a 'twist' because she does not sense a predictable ending; she is not a sophisticated reader of life's story. The narrator, on the other hand, is. With her bitter version of the past in the story-within-a-story, she harnesses the power of fiction in order to punish Douglas and, paradoxically, to set him free.

In some stories the narrative point of view may be unified and singular, and yet still perversely difficult and elusive, such as that of the contradictory first-person female 'I' in 'Tell Me Yes or No' (*Something*). Often, however, Munro achieves complexity even through a limited third-person narrator, such as the voice in 'Something I've Been Meaning to Tell You'.

These narrators, like the women of 'Hard-Luck Stories', are all polished storytellers with a sound grasp of their material and their audience, but they seem unable to avoid delivering mixed messages and laying false trails. Et, of 'Something I've Been Meaning to Tell You', has, as the title suggests, something to 'tell'. In one sense, this potential communication concerns her sister Char's imperfections; Et longs to reveal them to Char's widower, Arthur, who idolizes his beautiful wife as much in death as he did in life. But the 'something' Et has to tell is also directed, not at Arthur, but at the reader: the information that she may have brought about the death of Char by lying about Char's lover, Blaikie Noble. News of Blaikie's love affairs had once driven Char to attempt suicide; Et's wounding and invented story of his second betrayal of Char thus seems calculated to produce a similar—this time permanent—effect. The innocuous-seeming Et has had a crush on Arthur all along, and yearns to usurp Char's place in his life and heart. Et's control of the story is part of her power over both Char and Arthur, and she uses this to combat her disturbing discovery of passion and romance beneath the everyday surface of life.

After studying a photograph of Char, and comparing it with her sister's real-life appearance, Et concludes reluctantly that her sister is truly beautiful:

> This made Et understand, in some not entirely welcome way, that the qualities of legend were real, that they surfaced where and when you least expected. She had almost thought beautiful women were a fictional invention.

The irruption of the legendary into the everyday world is a common occurrence in Munro's fiction, one often signalled by allusions to the motifs and characters of fairy tale and myth. In 'Something' the love triangle of King Arthur, Guinevere, and Lancelot is evoked to counterpoint the Arthur, Char, and Et triangle. It is crafty Et who characterizes Arthur as King Arthur during a game of 'Who Am I':

'You should have been King Arthur,' Et said. 'King Arthur is your namesake.'

'I should have. King Arthur was married to the most beautiful woman in the world'.

'Ha,' said Et. 'We all know the end of that story.'

By invoking this legendary tale of passion and betrayal, Et calls attention to the Char-Blaikie relationship, thus diverting attention from the threat that she herself poses to the marriage.

A more self-conscious inventer of fictions is the first-person narrator of 'Tell Me Yes or No'. She too is adept at using stories to enact scenes of jealousy and revenge. This story opens with the line 'I persistently imagine you dead.' The 'you' is a sometime lover with whom the narrator communicates sporadically by letter, a shadowy male figure who becomes the immediate audience for the tissue of stories and inventions that unfolds as the narrator, ostensibly in search of the 'truth', imagines an irrevocable end to the affair:

> Would you like to know how I was informed of your death? I go into the faculty kitchen, to make myself a cup of coffee before my ten o'clock class. Dodie Charles who is always baking something has brought a cherry pound cake. (The thing we old pros know about, in these fantasies, is the importance of detail, solidity; yes, a cherry pound cake). It is wrapped in waxed paper and then in a newspaper. *The Globe and Mail*, not the local paper, that I would have seen.

This fantasy is self-consciously constructed; the narrator's parenthetical aside calls attention to her wish to flesh out the details, to anchor her story in 'reality'. But despite the seemingly solid ground of the cake and the *Globe and Mail*, the reader is soon lost in the maze of fantasy that follows. Recalling the past and pre-constructing the future, the narrator both celebrates and exorcises her own pain—a feeling she has been told is 'only possible if you looked backward to the past or forward to the future. . . .' The ultimate fantasy—the narrator's visit to her lover's 'widow' and the discovery that there has been a younger lover in his life—is studded with realistic detail, even anguished letters from the other 'other woman'. As the boundaries between invention and fact begin to blur, the reader is released from this unsettling state by the narrator's closing remarks:

> Never mind. I invented her. I invented you, as far as my purposes go.
> I invented loving you and I invented your death. I have my tricks and
> my trapdoors, too. I don't understand their workings at the present mo-
> ment, but I have to be careful. I won't speak against them.

The ending implies that the entire story is an unsent 'letter' to the lover, whose delinquency in letter-writing has led to the narrator's desire to kill him off, thus providing her with a valid excuse for the absent letters. Similarly, 'Something I've Been Meaning to Tell You' is constructed around another unsent message, the never-told 'something' that Et has up her sleeve. In both stories it is the potential power of the untold story—the unsent letter, the unsaid words—that fascinates. In 'Tell Me Yes or No' the title's demand for an answer is as much the reader's as it is the narrator's.

Munro's fiction is full of such storytellers—those who create private stories to assuage their own pain and guilt, or, as in 'Hard-Luck Stories', who actually tell their stories, using them as weapons in the skirmish of human relationships.

Occasionally Munro gives the construction of a story so central a place that it seems to be a work of metafiction (fiction about fiction). But although this term partly describes the effect of stories such as 'Material', 'Something I've Been Meaning to Tell You', 'Tell Me Yes or No', as well as 'Royal Beatings' (*Who Do You Think You Are?*), Munro is not one of the post-modern writers for whom metafiction is the last refuge of people bored by reality. Her stories do address head-on questions of the relation of art to reality, and of the natural process of story-making that suffuses the world. But fiction-making, though one of the most fascinating aspects of human nature, remains only one facet. While Munro uses some of the techniques and concerns of the post-modern movement, her stories resist their circularity because they do not discard content and meaning. They begin instead from the 'surface of life' that she considers such an important feature of her work.

In 'Material' the female narrator finds a published story written by her ex-husband, and is taken back to the incident in their past that gave Hugo the 'material' for his story. Juxtaposing the selfish, snobbish actions of the real Hugo with the unselfish gift that his fiction makes to the prostitute Dotty, the narrator is awed by the realization that Hugo is an artist after all.

> I was moved by Hugo's story: I was, I am, glad of it, and I am not moved by tricks. Or if I am, they have to be good tricks. Lovely tricks, honest tricks. There is Dotty lifted out of life and held in light, suspended in the marvelous clear jelly that Hugo has spent all his life learning how to make. It is an act of magic, there is no getting around it; it is an act, you might say, of a special, unsparing, unsentimental love.

In this simple praise of Hugo's artistry Munro provides what must surely be the most perceptive description of her own writing: of the vision that is 'unsparing' in both senses of the word. Munro is both ruthlessly thorough in her handling of character and place, and also unstinting in the kind and quality of love lavished on her own material. For the narrator of this story, however, a question still remains: does Hugo's retroactive gift to Dotty, her immortalization in the story, atone for his selfishness all those years ago, when he flooded her basement apartment by turning off the pump? His own peace of mind and sound sleep were more important to him than the safety of Dotty's material goods. Haunted by her own complicity in the incident, and by bitterness towards Hugo, the narrator continues to see Hugo as irresponsible. His disguise as the self-educated genius from the backwoods does not conceal his moral shortcomings, which are not atoned for by his undoubted talent as a writer.

> *This is not enough, Hugo. You think it is, but it isn't. You are mistaken Hugo.*

This story examines ethical issues surrounding the transformation of life through 'material' into art, but other Munro stories confront more basic questions about storytelling. In 'Royal Beatings' (*Who Do You Think You Are?*) origins, place, and the function of fiction in everyday life are analysed from a child's perspective. The beatings of 'Royal Beatings' occupy many levels of the story, beginning in the foreground where Rose is beaten and kicked by her father at the instigation of her stepmother Flo. But the sordid ritual takes place against a background of other beatings, more mysterious and fabulous, that have taken place on the wrong side of the tracks in West Hanratty, a straggling southwestern Ontario town. As a child, Rose had thrilled to the stories told by her step-mother Flo, of the Tydes, a local family, whose brutal father has made his name a byword for cruelty to his children. Munro's Tyde family—the deformed, dwarfish daughter Becky, the effeminate son, and the brutalized father—recalls the contorted vision of the American writers of Southern Gothic. There is a decidedly gothic cast to the tale of the public horsewhipping of Old Man Tyde that follows rumours of his imprisonment and impregnation of his crippled daughter. (A similarly gothic atmosphere pervades an earlier story, 'Executioners', in *Something I've Been Meaning To Tell You*.)

These horror stories occupy a privileged position in Flo's repertoire, and in Rose's imaginative grasp of her town's social history. Rose, however, cannot connect the 'shady melodramatic past' with the present reality, with Becky Tyde in the red shoes, or with her own humiliating beatings by a father temporarily transformed by hatred into a monster. But both the stories and the beating episodes have a certain ritual shape and function; both are trotted out to meet certain family situations, and to fill the gap between the palpable and the unmentionable in this 'most prudish' of families.

Story and beating are linked not just by function, but in Rose's imaginative reconstruction of a 'Royal beating':

> The word 'Royal' lolled on Flo's tongue, took on trappings. Rose had a need to picture things, to pursue absurdities, that was stronger than the need to stay out of trouble, and instead of taking this threat to heart she pondered: how is a beating royal? She came up with a tree-lined avenue, a crowd of formal spectators, some white horses and black slaves. Someone knelt, and the blood came leaping out like banners. An occasion both savage and splendid.

The delight in words and in the images they conjure up leads to one kind of story, born out of relish for the sound and meaning of words— 'the tumult of reason; the spark and spit of craziness.' Another kind of story emerges from the need to control and explain, and is invented by the pathetic old men loafing in front of the store. For them the planet Venus, spotted bright and low in the sky, has become a man-made object, 'an airship hovering over Bay City Michigan . . . lit by ten thousand electric light bulbs.' This fantasy is 'useful' in that it occupies the lonely men for a moment, and gives them a strong, if spurious, sense of connection with heavenly phenomena. Rose's story-picture of a 'Royal beating' is not useful or practical in the same sense; it does not even defer the punishment. But it does provide her with an imaginative release, one that bears her out of the kitchen setting of her own beatings, and beyond even the melodramatic past of horsewhipping in the town, to connect with the splendour and violence of a remote time and place. The transformation is akin to that effected by the stories of old Hat Nettelton, the town derelict and one of those who horsewhipped Old Man Tyde, interviewed on his 102nd birthday. In Hat's account the violence and disorder of the town of Hanratty have been ratified by the passing of time; horsewhipping and buggy races—compared by the interviewer to Roman chariot races—have been transmuted into something more dignified. But what decades of passing time have wrought naturally is effected in a few minutes by Rose's story; she transforms the mundane into the legendary, seeing the archetypes beneath the clutter of the everyday, and making literary order out of life's chaos.

In several other stories as well, Munro associates creative activity with a scene of surface chaos, suggesting that the disorder of life acts to free the imagination and liberate the mind into worlds of fantasy and word-play. In 'Winter Wind' (*Something*), for example, the high-school girl moves between poles of order and disorder, represented respectively by her grandmother's neat house in town, and her invalid mother's chaotic household in the country. The tidiness of the grandmother's house consists not only of physical order (Munro's details, such as 'ironed potholders', are devastatingly suggestive), but of moral and social order, a rigid sense of propriety that censors life's basic truths, and constructs a stultifying, but sturdy, carapace around the emotions.

The repressive order of Grandmother and Aunt Madge arrests the human understanding that flows from stories of the past. A rich fund of stories is possessed by the girl's invalid mother: 'She loved stories, particularly those full of tragedy and renunciation and queer turns of fate.' The older generation, on the other hand, suppress their stories, a response characterized for the narrator by the self-denying remark *'We must never speak of this again.'* The granddaughter hungers for the romantic story that haunts her grandmother's past: 'Even in that close-mouthed place, stories were being made. People carried their stories around with them. My grandmother carried hers, and nobody ever spoke of it to her face.' Eventually, with some trepidation, she reconstructs her own version of her grandmother's tragic renunciation of love, asking herself: 'And how is anybody to know . . . how am I to know what I claim to know?'

Stories bridge the gap between what can be admitted and what is unspeakable. For the granddaughter one avenue to understanding the past is the family photograph, in which a closed, patriarchal order is rendered imaginatively penetrable by the revealing disorder of the girls' dresses:

> The photograph was the sign and record of his achievement: respectability, moderate prosperity, mollified wife in a black silk dress, the well turned-out tall daughters.
>
> Though as a matter of fact their dresses looked frightful; flouncy and countrified.

From the small foothold provided by the awful dresses, the granddaughter enters the photograph, to recreate for herself a story of jealousy and romance, of a stubborn, secretive, and 'destructively romantic' past for her grandmother. In the end she affirms the validity of this exercise: '. . . I have not invented it, I really believe it. Without any proof I believe it, and so I must believe that we get messages another way, that we have connections that cannot be investigated, but have to be relied on.'

This intangible sense of connection underlies many of Munro's stories that feature a narrative quest for an understanding of the family past. 'Chaddeleys and Flemings' (*The Moons of Jupiter*) is divided into two sections; the first, which is called 'Connection', deals with connection not only in terms of family relationships, but in a less concrete sense 'that cannot be investigated'. The nature of the family connections is analysed through an anecdote about four cousins, the 'maiden ladies' who descend on a modest house in Dalgleish in Western Ontario for a reunion that is also a celebration of their shared privilege in being Chaddeleys. The narrator, a child at this time, sees them as connectors to a world of family history and heritage, and to stories of genteel origins in England:

> Connection. That was what it was all about. The cousins were a show in themselves, but they also provided a connection. A connection with the real, and prodigal, and dangerous, world.

Later the grown-up narrator will be confronted by her own inherited snobbery, when an older and reduced Cousin Iris comes to visit in Vancouver and is baited by the disapproving and social-climbing husband. An inheritor of the Chaddeleys' 'innocent snobbishness', the narrator has also acquired from her father's family another notion of superiority that is not based on social rank or false pretensions to gentility. The Chaddeley connection has given her shame and snobbery, along with a sense of fun, play, and disorder, while the Fleming family connection has left a legacy of pride, stubbornness, and close-mouthed solidarity. Formed by the two strains, she struggles to understand her own position as a teller of these family stories.

In the second part of the story, 'The Stone in the Field', the narrator explores her memories of the Scots farmers, the Flemings, especially her father's six unmarried reclusive sisters who are unchanging 'leftovers' from another generation. The story is structured around four contacts with the sisters and their retired way of life: a visit to their farm when the narrator was very small; a conversation with her father when he was dying; the discovery of an old newspaper clipping; and a final visit to the farm, long since sold out of the family, to search for the stone in the field.

From her father's recollections and the newspaper account of the death of Mr Black, a one-legged man on the Fleming farm, the narrator senses the existence of a story involving the sisters, something at odds with their drab life, perhaps even romantic. But lacking substance or detail, the narrator is reluctant to complete her storyteller's function:

> If I had been younger, I would have figured out a story. . . . Now I no longer believe that people's secrets are defined and communicable, or their feelings full-blown and easy to recognize.

In the end she resorts to facts, listing the everyday activities of the sisters' lives, and searching eventually for the one tangible bit of evidence in the case, the stone under which the mysterious one-legged Mr Black is said to be buried. Returning to the farm to examine the rock she vaguely remembers from her childhood, she meets a new generation of farmers, solid, commercial, and successful. Not surprisingly, they have done away with the stone in the corner of the field, whose boundaries have likely been altered. The story, faded by the agency of time, sinks back into the land along with its corroborative stone. Whereas the young narrator in 'Winter Wind' wrested the story of past romance from a photograph and from two uncompromising old women, the relationship in 'The Stone in the Field' between past and present, between story and storyteller, is much quieter, even quiescent. The lineaments of the story are suggested, but her Fleming inheritance prevents the narrator from embroidering or elaborating.

'The Stone in the Field' is one of Munro's finest stories, its beauty inhering in the delicacy and restraint with which the romance and melodrama are treated. A strong sense of the physical reality of these reclusive sisters and the pain they experienced through 'human contact' lingers in the reader's mind, and if a 'story' lies buried under the stony fields and lye-scrubbed floors of the farm on Mount Hebron, we are content to leave it there. Munro's tact in handling her story satisfies the reader that the narrator knows when to stop: 'I carry something of them around in me. But the boulder is gone.'

An early story from *Dance of the Happy Shades*, 'The Peace of Utrecht' (first published in *The Tamarack Review* in 1960), covers ground similar to that of 'The Stone in the Field'. A young mother, Helen, returns to the small town of her childhood, and makes her peace with a family inheritance from which she had earlier fled. Munro's evocation of life in the genteel side streets of a small Ontario town (here called Jubilee) is masterful:

I drove up the main street—a new service station, new stucco front on the Queen's Hotel—and turned into the quiet, decaying side streets where old maids live, and have birdbaths and blue delphiniums in their gardens. The big brick houses that I knew, with their wooden verandahs and gaping dark-screened windows, seemed to me plausible but unreal. (Anyone to whom I have mentioned the dreaming, sunken feeling of those streets wants to take me out to the north side of town where there is a new soft-drink bottling plant, some new ranch-style houses and a Tastee-Freez.)

Like the narrator of 'The Stone in the Field', Helen searches the territory of the past for understanding. Her sister Maddy, who stayed behind to look after an invalid mother, has endured a 'dim world of continuing disaster'. Now that the mother is dead, Maddy wants to savour her freedom, but cannot—crying out at the end of the story to know *why* she cannot. In part two of the story Helen visits her two old aunts, keepers of the past and its guilt. Maddy and Helen, Aunt Annie and Auntie Lou, represent paired possibilities for small-town women of different generations. Munro creates a compelling portrait of the two old women, with their dark, polished house, their rag rugs, and their 'shapeless print dresses trimmed with rickrack and white braid'. Helen senses uncharacteristic 'signs of disagreement' between the aunts, and it is only when Aunt Annie broaches to Helen the subject of her mother's death that she understands the source of the discord: Auntie Lou 'had a dislike of certain rituals of emotionalism; such a conversation could never take place with her about.' But further discord emerges from Aunt Annie's revelations about the terrible nature of the death: a hint of blame against Maddy—the sister who stayed behind to care for their mother—is offered to the sister who left. What Helen learns from this conversation is the finality of the 'tradition of circumlocution' through which these women communicate. She must finally agree with Maddy that nobody 'speaks the same language'. Helen, on finding an old school notebook in a drawer and seeing the words 'The Peace of Utrecht, 1713, brought an end to the War of the Spanish Succession', had momentarily felt that the pieces of her old life were lying around her 'waiting to be picked up again'. But like that fragile 'peace', composed of multiple agreements made by many parties, her peace with her sister is illusionary: 'at heart we reject each other, and as for that past we make so much of sharing, we do not really share it at all.'

Munro's stories often deal with generational conflict. Discord between mothers and daughters is sometimes complicated by another family member—a grandmother, a sibling, an aunt, cousin, or uncle. Such a pattern underlies both 'Winter Wind' and a closely related story, 'The Ottawa Valley' (*Something*). The latter story, which Munro has said is more autobiographical than the rest of her work, portrays a daughter striving to understand her mother, and struggling to retell her story in a manner that is just to both. We see a sulky daughter who resents her mother's illness, but also fears losing her and exorcises that fear by demanding that her mother promise she will get well, and a vain mother with pretensions to gentility and a stern moral exterior that represses the lighter side of life. But the narrator also illuminates her mother through the agency of Aunt Dodie, the mother's jilted country cousin whose house is bare of furniture, yet filled with song, jokes, and stories. Aunt Dodie relates a hilarious, slightly bawdy story of a long-ago prank played by the two girls on a young male farm-hand that reflects an unsuspected carefree side of her mother that the daughter cannot reconcile with the proper woman she knows. The end of the story finds Munro's narrator dissatisfied with the order of her own creation, lamenting the inadequacy of its representation. She finds that she cannot sum up her mother, and thereby 'get rid of her' in order to be free of her closeness, which still 'weighs everything down'.

Other stories that deal with the distance between generations and the possibility of bridging it through storytelling include 'Marrakesh' (*Something*), 'A Queer Streak' (*The Progress of Love*), and, indirectly, 'Miles City, Montana' (*Progress*). In this story the young mother, travelling through Miles City on her way from British Columbia to Ontario, is driven by the near-drowning of her little daughter, Meg, to recall a drowning incident from her own childhood. Her memory of the past is vivid with sensory detail, although she realizes that it may be more imagined than real—the green slime in the nostrils of the drowned Steve Gauley, for example—but her memory of the strong emotion she experienced at the funeral is authentic. (Munro uses the selfsame detail about a drowned boy to convey Et's revulsion against her sister's sexuality in 'Something I've Been Meaning to Tell You'.) The pure sense of blame, betrayal, and hatred felt by the little girl towards adults is rooted in a perceptual severance between child and adult that is irreversible. The child accuses her own decent and charitable parents and all the grown-ups present—with the sole exception of the drowned boy's father—of complicity in the drowning, and of hypocrisy in the pious church service:

> When I stood apart from my parents at Steve Gauley's funeral and watched them, and had this new, unpleasant feeling about them, I thought that I was understanding something about them for the first time. It was a deadly serious thing. I was understanding that they were implicated. Their big, stiff, dressed-up bodies did not stand between me and sudden death, or any kind of death. They gave consent. So it seemed. They gave consent to the death of children and to my death not by anything they said or thought but by the very fact that they had made children—they had made me.

But the boy's father is 'let off the hook' because he is not a parent who promises protection or engages in any of the ritual manifestations of grief, 'oozing religion and dishonor'. After Meg's near-drowning in the Miles City municipal pool, the young mother finds herself on the other side of the picture, savouring a 'trashy' pleasure in her brush with catastrophe, and remembering how close the line was for a child between adult helplessness and adult complicity.

The story ends with one of Munro's wonderful catalogues of adjectives, often used in her fiction to pinpoint the elusive, various nature of human beings and their judgements:

> So we went on, with the two in the back seat trusting us, because of no choice, and we ourselves trusting to be forgiven in time what first had to be seen and condemned by those children: whatever was flippant, arbitrary, careless, callous—all our natural, and particular, mistakes.

The structure of 'Miles City, Montana'—with its paired events from past and present, and the meditative, half-guilty voice linking events and pondering their joint implications—is typical of

Munro's later stories. Particularly in her early work, Munro wrote a tighter story, in which discovery by the protagonist revealed a hidden awareness, as in 'Images' (*Dance of the Happy Shades*), which ends with a moment of clarity rather than questioning. The title suggests a story with an episodic quality that will unfold in a set of stop-action photographs. To some extent this is the case, as the narrator presents images of her childhood and of the family disruption surrounding her mother's pregnancy, particularly the intrusion of a practical nurse, the fearful Mary McQuade. The discoveries made by this little girl are two-fold. First they concern Mary McQuade herself, who with her strange smell, foreign habits, and coarse practical jokes signals something completely new in the child's universe:

> I doubted that she was asked to come. She came, and cooked what she liked and rearranged things to suit herself, complaining about draughts, and let her power loose in the house. If she had never come my mother would never have taken to her bed.

What is most frightening to the child is that her parents welcome Mary and seem resigned to the gritty and depressing side of life that she heralds. But even stranger revelations await, when the child is taken by her father on a tour of his trap-lines. What begins as a spring outing soon becomes a nightmare experience, involving a meeting with an axe-carrying eccentric—the archetypal bogeyman—and a visit to his eerie underground dwelling. Carried home, asleep, by her father, she wakes up to find that the seemingly epic journey has merely taken them around in a circle, and that they are facing home again. But they are now looking at the house from a new and challenging angle: 'We had come around in a half-circle and there was the side of the house that nobody saw in winter. . . .'

Waking from one reality into another, the child is introduced to the secret nature of the grown-up world and, having been warned by her father not to 'mention' the axe, she has gained a small toe-hold in that world, a vantage point from which the terrible Mary McQuade is diminished in power:

> Like the children in fairy stories who have seen their parents make pacts with terrifying strangers, who have discovered that our fears are based on nothing but the truth, but who come back fresh from marvelous escapes and take up their knives and forks, with humility and good manners, prepared to live happily ever after—like them, dazed and powerful with secrets, I never said a word.

Munro considers these closed endings less attractive than her more open ones: 'Mostly in my stories I like to look at what people don't understand.'

The title story of *Dance of the Happy Shades* exhibits a similar sense of discovery in the ending. The narrative technique is *not* discursive or diversionary, but is a highly orchestrated approach to the main scene of a piano recital, where a handicapped child produces, miraculously, not a 'performance', as the other children do, but real music. The decaying, genteel Miss Marsalles—one of Munro's finest creations—is revealed through her furnishings, her clothes, and the refined refreshments she serves. At her annual recital grown women can relive the 'ceremonies of childhood' that only Miss Marsalles seems never to outgrow. She has carried her innocence into her old age. Her matter-of-fact acceptance of miracles is a disruption of the adult social order, where the retarded child's musical talent seems somehow to be 'not *in good taste*'. But Miss Marsalles's innocence emerges as a kind of gift, in a story that is about gifts and the manner of their reception. They can be taken grudgingly—as are the prim, paper-wrapped recital gifts for the unappreciative children—or they can be accepted as innocently and naturally as Miss Marsalles accepts the musical talent of the handicapped girl.

Many of the stories in *Dance of the Happy Shades* are directly concerned with a child's awareness of, and adaptation to, an adult world of social and moral etiquette. In 'Boys and Girls' (a story that was later televised) a young farm girl must learn that she is 'only' a girl, and that the role comes with gifts of feeling as well as limitations of scope. 'Red Dress' presents an older girl, at the adolescent stage where a longing for the safe 'boundaries of childhood' may occur. Munro nostalgically embalms, and at the same time gently satirizes, the rituals of the high-school dance in a small town, showing the teenager's longing for, and fear of, 'social adjustment', and her shameful delight at being 'rescued' by a dance partner from the ignominy of girls' company in the washroom.

In this collection, too, is a story told by one of Munro's rare male speakers. Despite the male narrative voice, 'Thanks for the Ride' is really about Lois, the small-town girl who goes along for a summer joyride. Behind her mask of indifference and cynicism lies a volcanic sexuality, portrayed by Munro as a kind of gift, an act of mystical surrender. At the end of the story the careful reader is absorbed in decoding the layers of meaning contained in the male narrator's presentation of Lois's parting remark: 'And then we heard the female voice calling after us, the loud, crude, female voice, abusive and forlorn:"Thanks for the ride!"' The tone seems to deepen from sarcasm, through gratitude, relief and remorse, to despair and a kind of resignation.

Having tried her hand at the longer form of the novel with *Lives of Girls and Women* (1971)—which nevertheless is composed of linked stories—Munro returned to the short story proper with *Something I've Been Meaning to Tell You*. In these thirteen stories, she demonstrates the maturity of both her artistic vision and her craft. All of her most characteristic techniques and themes are represented here: the complex narrator, the diversionary narrative strategy, the divination of the hidden self in the concealed past, the use of documents and photographs as tools in the search for the truth behind stories. The canvas of these stories is a crowded one, but typically Munro chooses to·subordinate plot and character to what she calls a 'climate' in the story—the precariously smug atmosphere of the boy's funeral in 'Memorial', the glorious freedom and promise of the discovered boat in 'The Found Boat.' In many of the stories Munro appears to be testing and questioning the methods of her own craft, challenging both her material (in 'Material'), and her right to shape it ('Ottawa Valley', 'Winter Wind').

The next collection, *Who Do You Think You Are?*, combines mastery of the short-story form with an attempt at a longer fictional form, the linked-story cycle. Munro's subject, however, remains substantially the territory of the lives of girls and women, that of Rose and her stepmother, Flo, of West Hanratty. In the United States the book appeared under a different title (*The Beggar Maid: Stories of Flo and Rose*) because the American publisher felt that the question 'Who do you think you are?' would have no resonance for an American audience unaccustomed to such ironic reminders of the power of social hierarchy.

The stories follow roughly the growth of Rose from a child in 'Royal Beatings', through adolescence—'White Swans', 'The Beggar Maid'—to middle age and a reversal of roles between Rose and Flo ('Spelling'). Some stories are left tantalizingly open-ended ('Mischief', 'Simon's Luck'), while others ('Half a Grapefruit') depict with completion and finality Rose's confrontation with the wounding social hierarchy of school and town. The often-anthologized 'Wild Swans' tells the story of Rose's first solo train trip to Toronto. On this epochal journey she is molested by a clergyman in the next seat, and experiences conflicting feelings of pleasure and repulsion, shame and curiosity. The title story, the last of ten, ends the collection significantly on a note of question and challenge. Milton Homer in this story is one of Munro's most accomplished depictions of a small-town eccentric, tolerated and even cherished by a community where, paradoxically, the social pecking order is ruthlessly maintained.

The Moons of Jupiter (1982) shows a return to the format of discrete stories, and presents a great variety of settings—Australia, Toronto, and New Brunswick, as well as the more usual southwestern Ontario. The eleven stories, however, are drawn together by the recurrence of a middle-aged female protagonist, single and searching for some connection in a difficult and sometimes hostile world. In 'Dulse', on an island off New Brunswick Lydia meets three very different men: a boy, a man in vigorous middle age, and an old man, Mr Stanley, who lives for and through his admiration for the writer Willa Cather. What Lydia takes from the schematic encounter is aptly suggested by the dried seaweed of the story's title—a 'sly' warmth that comes from a gift of the self, quietly given and pleasurably received.

The title story of the collection, 'The Moons of Jupiter', contains a similar female figure, this one caught in her dual role as mother of two grown daughters, and as daughter of a hospitalized and dying father. A visit to the planetarium, which provides the title reference, transports the woman to a realm of 'innumerable repetition', where her position between the older and the younger generations is put in perspective. The bedridden father entertains himself by remembering snatches of poetry, coming up with a half-remembered phrase that echoes his daughter's experience of vastness and diminution in the planetarium:

> 'Shoreless seas'. . . . That's what was going through my head last night. But do you think I could remember what kind of seas?. . . That's always the way, isn't it? It's not all that surprising. I ask my mind a question. The answer's there, but I can't see all the connections my mind's making to get it.

The operation of the mind is very much like the operation of the story; in both, meaning creeps in at the corners, when least expected and in the most unlikely places. With its symbolic suggestions and mythological allusiveness, the title hints at this peripheral significance but does not yield any watertight system of meaning. As in so many of Munro's stories, what lingers is a sense of the mystery of connection in life.

The stories in Munro's latest collection, *The Progress of Love* (1986), retain much of the diversity and the enigma of those in *The Moons of Jupiter*. Several exhibit the diversionary narrative that swerves between events past and present—'Monsieur Les Deux Chapeaux', for example, and 'The Progress of Love' (which has also been dramatized on television). First published in *The New Yorker* (where many of Munro's recent stories have appeared), the title story, like so much of Munro's fiction since the early seventies, takes a familiar narrative detour back into the past lives of characters in quest of understanding of present situations. The narrator, Fame, explores the life of her mother, Marietta, and the ravages wrought upon it by her grandmother's near-suicide. After seeing her mother standing with the noose around her neck, Marietta can never again love or forgive her father for his treatment of her mother. This hatred colours her life and she warns Fame against it:

> Hatred is always a sin, my mother told me. Remember that. One drop of hatred in your soul will spread and discolor everything like a drop of black ink in white milk.

But Fame is puzzled to discover that there is another version of the story of her grandmother's 'hanging': her Aunt Beryl remembers the event as much less serious and she has *not* kept a legacy of hatred. Furthermore, Beryl did keep the money left her by the father, whereas Marietta burned hers in the kitchen stove. The story contains a central mystery in the discrepancy between two versions of an event so important as to change family lives for generations. A further mystery is hinted at in the title—an odd title for a story that is apparently about hatred. But Munro's title is ambiguous in its reference, as so many of her later titles are. 'Progress' is not merely a movement forward from a time when 'love and grudges could be growing underground', but also a formal procession, orderly and ceremonious, including many diverse characters in its composition, and touching many states and persons in its passage. Notable in this 'progress' is the steadfast love Fame's father shows for Marietta, and Fame's love for them both. In this sense, the progress of love—indirect but relentless, various but orderly—is the subject of *all* Munro's fiction.

5

MARGARET ATWOOD

Although better known as a novelist and a distinguished poet, Margaret Atwood also excels in the writing of short stories. In addition to her two collections, *Dancing Girls* (1977) and *Bluebeard's Egg* (1983), *Murder in the Dark* (1983) contains short prose pieces that skirt the edge of the short-story form without declaring absolute allegiance; the difficulty of categorizing these engaging and sometimes whimsical pieces is suggested by the book's subtitle, *Short Fictions and Prose Poems*. But even in the first two collections Atwood continually tests the boundaries of the short story, offering her readers ample opportunity to flex the muscles of the imagination.

Atwood's stories are narrated in a variety of voices, from varied points of view, and are set in an array of geographical locations. Their most pronounced tone is that of a visionary discontent—the voice of a narrator who sees, describes with great acuity, and understands human dilemmas, but is powerless to affect the outcome. At their most satirical they feature a highly educated and sensitive narrator who seems bemused by the small vagaries of human nature and pop culture but is lucidly aware of the implications of global issues. Even her first-person narrators evince an obsessive sense of their own difference from other people, and of their detachment from the world. Often the stories appear to seek the alignment of the reader with such a character, making the experience of reading seem like an entry into an 'other' world where the certainty and solidity of the familiar world are inverted. Language itself becomes one of these 'other' worlds, a difficult and dangerous territory. But the abrupt inversions and reversals of perspective in the stories often culminate in a visionary experience that provides an almost mystical closure.

Nevertheless in the first collection, *Dancing Girls*, some of the stories seem far removed from mystical experience of any kind, sharing a solid, unromantic female protagonist, differently named, but recognizably the same type. This clumsy and myopic anti-heroine (Christine, in 'The Man from Mars', or Ann of 'Dancing Girls') conceals her body (usually unfashionably ample) in layers of bulky clothing. The protagonist of 'Hair Jewellery', for example, describes her wearing apparel: 'Most of my clothes were the same, they were all too big, perhaps I believed that if my clothes were large and shapeless, if they formed a sort of tent around me, I would be less visible.' The odd clothes are assumed as a disguise, but soon tighten into a skin, becoming the most real and memorable part of her experience:

> . . . I resurrect myself through clothes. In fact it's impossible for me to remember what I did, what happened to me, unless I can remember what I was wearing, and every time I discard a sweater or a dress I am discarding a part of my life. I shed identities like a snake . . .

Far from being shackled by their excess clothing, these tweedy, swaddled women (present also in 'Under Glass' and 'Polarities') seem always poised for transformation, by way of some creative snake-like shedding of the layers of skin, or, more romantically, by emerging like a butterfly. Christine, Ann, Louise, and the nameless narrators of 'Hair Jewellery' and 'Under Glass' are all cocoon women, though the transformation they await promises horror more often than beauty. Like the poet at the end of 'Lives of the Poets', these mummified women anticipate a moment of apocalyptic transformation, when they will emerge as they really are: 'No sweet identity, she will clench herself against it. She will step across the stage, words coiled, she will open her mouth and the room will explode in blood.'

This sanguinary ending is unusual, however. More often Atwood uses her anti-heroines to deflate threatening moods of romance, tragedy, terror, and horror. In 'The Man from Mars', for example, the hefty and athletic Christine functions, with her tennis dress and tennis racket, as an antidote to the creeping mystery and potential terror surrounding the seedy little foreigner who follows her around. Louise, the half-mad heroine of 'Polarities', possesses a similarly practical and athletic wardrobe, but what humanizes her for her hapless friend Morrison is not her corduroys, but her fuzzy blue bedroom slippers. Most adept at puncturing the mood of horror or romance, however, is Estelle of 'Rape Fantasies'. With her kleenexes, her Neo-Citran, and her plastic lemon, she effectively neutralizes all her fantasized rape attempts, reducing terror to slapstick.

These deflationary heroines manage to deny the possibility of romance, horror, and terror in everyday life. But the stridency of the denial suggests the proximity of such melodramatic events and transformations. Whereas the everyday world in Alice Munro's stories often harbours another world of legend and romance, in Atwood's stories the everyday simply disguises the horrific, and her cocooned heroines are just one feature of a gothic vision that includes the possibility of ghastly metamorphoses in people, objects, and words. Although her heroines evade such transformations, they are simultaneously fascinated by them. Fear and fascination blend in an atmosphere best described as 'metamorphobic', a word that playfully suggests the pervasive fear of monstrous transformation either in oneself or in others.

Atwood sometimes plays consciously with notions of the Gothic (in 'Hair Jewellery' for example, where the protagonist is a graduate student in Literature), but usually its elements are concealed, until they spring out unexpectedly from moments in the lives of ordinary people who are both deformed and transformed by strong emotion. Despite a preoccupation with the thin boundary between the mundane and the monstrous, however, the stories are not melodramatic. They exhibit, in fact, a remarkably cool tone, a distinct Atwoodian 'voice' composed in equal parts of irony, self-deprecation, and disembodied detachment.

Atwood's characteristic narrative point of view is presented by a third person of limited omniscience. In some stories this limited perspective seems at one with the main character, and modulates into a form of indirect interior monologue (for example, with Alma of 'The Salt Garden'). In the stories in *Dancing Girls* that are told from a first-person point of view—'Under Glass', 'The Grave of the Famous Poet', 'Rape Fantasies', 'Hair Jewellery', and 'Lives of the Poets'—the tone ranges from the meditative confessional of 'Under Glass' or 'The Grave of the Famous Poet' to the naïvely garrulous and deceptively debunking tone of 'Rape Fantasies'.

Popular with anthologists, 'Rape Fantasies' offers a monologue by Estelle that begins with her description of an episode of lunch-room talk among her girl-friends at work. The subject of rape fantasies, introduced by Chrissy as a trendy, slightly titillating topic, soon becomes a forum for Estelle's own anti-fantasies. She deflates Chrissy's tepid fantasy of bathtub rape with a reminder of the natural hazards: '. . . you might get bubbles up your nose . . . from the deep breathing.' Her own fantasies prove to be unromantic and unerotic, centring on bumbling, essentially human would-be rapists, who are ineffectual and pathetic. By introducing mundane details from reality into her rape fantasies, Estelle eliminates the erotic element—the received dialectic of mastery and surrender—replacing it with a domestic element of human need and mutual succour. One of her fantasized attackers is foiled by a squirt from a plastic lemon, after he has obligingly consented to hold the jumbled contents of Estelle's overflowing purse while she scrabbles through its depths to retrieve this ludicrous weapon.

Humour dominates the story up to this point, as Atwood spoofs the pop psychology of glossy magazines and the absurdities they instil in the self-images of gullible women. But the reader soon realizes that Estelle is relating the lunch-room episode to someone else, an unnamed shadowy listener. A sinister element creeps into her compulsive monologue when it becomes evident that the listener is male, and that Estelle is new in town, lonely, and hanging out in a bar. This information adds a *frisson* to her naïve recitation of received opinion on rape:

> The funny thing about these fantasies is that the man is always some-one I don't know, and the statistics in the magazines, well, most of them anyway, they say it's often someone you do know, at least a little bit . . . or someone you just met, who invites you up for a drink. . . .

The silence on the other side of the monologue becomes extremely disturbing, and the humour of Estelle's fantasies of rapists who have leukemia and terrible colds—which are ultimately not rape fantasies at all, but women's dreams of comfortable companionship and domestic happiness—recedes, and she begins to seem doomed. While admiring her refusal to conform to a sexist stereotype, the reader is made uncomfortable by Estelle's naïvety in pouring out her heart to a sinister stranger in a bar. Towards the end of the story she offers an increasing amount of editorial comment—'I don't know why I'm telling you all this . . .'—that calls attention to her growing unease and incipient awareness of the unsuitability of her confession.

When Estelle begins to prattle of 'real rape fantasy', the story crosses the border from the humorous to the horrific. The comforts of fantasy are invaded by the unpredictability of the 'real'. This withdrawal of certainties through narrative control is one of Atwood's most characteristic and effective devices, and is also used in the opening story in *Dancing Girls*, 'The War in the Bathroom'.

Divided diary-like into daily entries, this story begins as a first-person record of the activities of another woman to whom the narrative voice condescends: 'She is quite strong for her age; . . . She wanted some ice cream but I told her to get a package of frozen peas instead.' But the reader soon realizes that 'I' and 'she' occupy the same body; they represent a mind-body split, a radical fragmentation of an old woman's self. The 'I' dominates the 'she' and makes clear that there is antagonism and even downright hostility between them that is mirrored in the narrator's paranoid attitude towards the world outside.

The old woman suspects everyone around her of conspiracy, and reveals on the opening pages of the story that she has changed boarding houses because of her fear. At the new boarding house she begins a campaign for ownership of the communal bathroom, taking as her main opponent the innocuous old man downstairs. The war ends in a sinister victory for the old woman, as she locks the door and listens to the old man falling down the stairs:

> She made a movement to get out of the bathtub but I told her to stay where she was. She lay in the bathtub, staring at her pink toes floating on

the surface of the water, while I listened. I knew the bathroom door was securely locked.
For the time being I have won.

Atwood introduces into the story an eerie analogy for the psychic division represented by the narrative voice. Another user of the bathroom appears to be a woman with two voices, 'one high and querulous, the other an urgent whisper'. This binary figure turns out on investigation *not* to be one woman talking to herself, but actually two women:

I know now that there are two women. The one that whispers is an old lady, very thin, with small dark eyes that are like holes in her head. She was wrapped in a blanket and was being carried by the other woman [who is] heavy set and muscular, with a round vacuous face.

The narrator reveals that her other self 'was upset' by this incident, and declares, 'I will never allow her to live like that.' Although she is upset by the symbolic joining of two persons to form a unit—one directing, one carrying out directions—the narrator herself presides over a grotesque pairing that does not join but splits the self in two. The story offers many hints that the division between 'I' and 'she' is not merely a split between a well-preserved mind and its ageing body, but a much more disturbing and radical breach that strands all impulses of affect, sentiment, and human rapprochement on the subordinate 'she' side. Thus the 'victory' at the end of the story is only partly a rout of the old man downstairs; more sinisterly, the narrator's assertion, 'For the time being I have won', denotes her victory over the 'she' side of her personality—a conquering of the last vestiges of human feeling within herself.

This story of psychic unwholeness sets the tone for the rest of *Dancing Girls*. Another victim of psychic division is Louise of 'Polarities'. Isolated in a prairie winter, wrestling with the intricacy of Blake's poetry, the graduate student Louise loses her grip on one reality and invents another. She seizes on a scheme of division within the prairie city—'The city is polarized north and south; the river splits it in two; the poles are the gas plant and the power plant'—and tries to convince her American friend Morrison that they have a mission to unite the city. After Louise is taken to a mental institution, Morrison begins to find her more attractive, and to see her visions as more and more sane. Louise, he says, has 'taken as real what the rest of us pretend is only metaphorical'. With the crucial word 'pretend', Atwood plants the seeds of a subversive revision of the literal and the metaphorical, particularly as applied to literary and social theories of the polarities of Canadian culture. Certainly Louise's 'private system' does not differ markedly in its language from many other theories—of east-west division, of Northern orientation, of symbolic unification of a large and divided country.

At the end of 'Polarities', Morrison visits the winter-bound zoo and, gazing at the wolves in their almost invisible pen, is afforded one of Atwood's ambiguous visionary moments. As he swoons into the snow, the landscape seems to open before him; he is received into communion with the place that had relentlessly debarred him. For Morrison, it is clear that the only solution to this land and this society is madness. Louise, therefore, has made the sane choice in ceasing to 'pretend' that real divisions are only metaphorical, and has succumbed to the polarities within herself and her society.

A much more positive depiction of psychic division occurs in 'Giving Birth', the last story in *Dancing Girls*. Like Louise, and like the old woman in 'The War in the Bathroom', the narrator of 'Giving Birth' is hallucinatory. The experience of giving birth is attributed to another woman, whom the narrator calls Jeannie, and from whom she carefully distances herself by name, hair colour, and other details, although the narrator herself has recently given birth. To further complicate the division of the self, she provides Jeannie with a shadow self, a disadvantaged woman, nameless, mute, and long-suffering, whose unwanted pregnancy coincides with Jeannie's own deliberate act of giving birth.

Despite her distancing and her division, however, this narrator possesses a resource alien to both Louise and the old woman in the bathroom—she has a powerful respect for, and simultaneous distrust of, language. The sense that language itself is a dangerous and powerful element, one that can either support or swallow its user, originates in Atwood's poetry, but recurs in many of her short stories. For Atwood all language is a distortion, a limited and slippery medium that takes a sly revenge on its users and abusers. The narrator of 'Giving Birth', aware of this lurking duplicity, challenges words to give up their secrets, musing on the meaning of the phrase 'giving birth':

> But who gives it? And to whom is it given? . . . No one ever says *giving death*, although they are in some ways the same, events, not things.

This narrator seems to wade through language as through an almost palpable medium, using liquid or semi-liquid metaphors throughout. Here, as elsewhere in her writing, Atwood depicts language through an image of a pool, a medium with both surface and depth, although the line between them can be deceptive and therefore dangerous. This image is invariably accompanied by a warning against using the pool as a mirror; to look into the water for your own reflection, to look to language for an absolute reflection of reality—both are mistakes. The narrator of 'Giving Birth' articulates the danger:

> . . . in language there are always these 'points', these reflections; this is what makes it so rich and sticky, this is why so many have disappeared beneath its dark and shining surface, why you should never try to see your own reflection in it; you will lean over too far, a strand of your hair will fall in and come out gold, and, thinking it is gold all the way down, you yourself will follow. . . .

The tempting transformations of the self offered by literature beckon to this narrator too. While her baby naps, she tells us, 'I am writing this story.' She uses her character, Jeannie, to 'bring myself closer to something that time has already made distant'. Both Jeannie and her narrator sense the inadequacy of words to an experience that is beyond words, an 'event of the body', and so indescribable. If giving birth exists beyond words, it does so in a realm of mystery, where visions are made; Jeannie hopes desperately that such a vision will be granted. At the end of the story, disobeying doctor's orders, and too soon on her feet, Jeannie wrests her vision painfully from the experience, watching through the hospital window as the neighbouring buildings waver, crumple, and disintegrate. Her vision of the transparency and fragility of the material world is reminiscent of Morrison's vision at the end of 'Polarities'. Both characters *earn* their visions, by being receptive to a world apart from the orderly, rational word-oriented world. They actively seek out the world beyond words, taking the plunge beneath the surface of language, and of rational experience, and finding that drowning too can bring a kind of understanding.

Such visionary endings also occur in Atwood's second volume of short stories, *Bluebeard's Egg*. Yvonne, the ascetic artist in 'The Sunrise', extracts her own morning vision painfully, and at great sacrifice. A solitary figure, almost hermit-like, she pursues her artistic goals, along with the male subjects she needs to attain them, with single-minded dedication. Outwardly she appears totally self-sufficient, but her personal life is attenuated. Atwood uses a detached third-person voice to show dispassionately the true end of Yvonne's hermit-like existence, the worship of and surrender to a visionary excess in the moment of sunrise. In 'Scarlet Ibis', too, the climax of the story is a moment beyond words—the vision of the rare red birds against the swampy tropical sky:

> 'Birds ahoy,' said one of the men in baseball caps, and pointed, and then there were the birds all right, flying through the reddish light, right on cue, first singly, then in flocks of four or five, so bright, so fluorescent that they were like painted flames. They settled into the trees, screaming hoarsely. It was only the screams that revealed them as real birds.

For the tourist Christine this experience is one of transport in the metaphysical sense; she is taken up into another world, given a glimpse of its existence behind the real one. Like Morrison, and the mother in 'Giving Birth', she sees herself anew:

> Don took hold of Christine's hand, a thing he had not done for some time; but Christine, watching the birds, noticed this only afterwards. She felt she was looking at a picture, of exotic flowers or of red fruit growing on trees, evenly spaced, like the fruit in the gardens of medieval paintings, solid, clear-edged, in primary colours. On the other side of the fence was another world, not real but at the same time more real than the one on this side, the men and women in their flimsy clothes and aging bodies, the decrepit boat. Her own body seemed fragile and empty, like blown glass.

A more complex and curious visionary moment is afforded to Alma in 'The Salt Garden' (*Bluebeard's Egg*). Alma is subject to episodes, seizures, in which a 'sudden white flash' precipitates the crumbling of the outside world and Alma's loss of consciousness. Struggling for a meaning behind her experience, Alma searches for the right word, rejecting 'hallucination,' 'acid flash', 'epilepsy', and 'schizophrenia'. No explanation seems adequate, and Alma concludes that she is part of a collective, prophetic vision of the nuclear-aided end of the world. Not an activist herself, she revels in her passivity:

> Never before has her life felt so effortless, as if all responsibility has been lifted from her. She floats. There's a commercial on television, for milk, she thinks, that shows a man riding at the top of a wave on a surfboard: moving, yet suspended, as if there is no time. This is how Alma feels: removed from time. Time presupposes a future.

At the end of the story, when Alma has just received the brush-off from her lover, she experiences simultaneously another 'obliterating flash of light'. Recovering from her black-out, and contemplating the end of the relationship, Alma has the gently horrific vision of death and emptiness that ends the story:

> Right now the salt drifts down behind her eyes, falling like snow, down through the ocean, past the dead coral, gathering on the branches of the salt tree that rises from the white crystal dunes below it. Scattered on the underwater sand are the bones of many small fish. It is so beautiful. Nothing can kill it. After everything is over, she thinks, there will still be salt.

Here Atwood transforms the salt garden of Alma's kitchen chemistry—a domestic wonder made for the amusement of Alma's daughter, with a spoon, a glass, a string, and a salt solution—into a prophetic vision of a world returned to its base elements. The salt garden of the final paragraph is beautiful, clean, and pure; it has been purged, purified, and killed in the process. If this is the salt of life, it has lost its savour.

Another vision with a direct, critical relevance to the real world is Anne's in the earlier story 'Dancing Girls'. The city-bound Ann, a student of Urban Design, dreams of perfect green spaces that she will learn to create, 'with water flowing through them, and trees. . . . And no formal flower beds.' The problem with Ann's vision, as with Alma's, is the lack of human life: 'she could see the vistas, the trees and the streams or canals, quite clearly, but she could never visualize the people. Her green spaces were always empty.'

As in 'The Salt Garden', the vision returns to close the story; a disillusioned Ann realizes the impossibility of her pure, clean place, devoid of nuisance people like the landlady's children. Into the dream she is reluctantly relinquishing, creeps a stately, colourful troop of people, in their 'native costumes', a Unesco-card vision of the diverse but united world. Among them are the dancing girls of the story's title: they are not the hired whores recruited by the lonely foreign student in the next flat, but ordinary women, in the landlady's attire, all of them 'sedately dancing'. The image of the dance suggests a state of orderly freedom, the tamed wildness for which the Urban Designer strives. But it is an image of an impossible compromise; the Dutch smiles, the mauve scuffies worn by the dancers cannot easily be reconciled with the passion and abandon implied by the term 'dancing girls'. Ann knows that her dream is 'cancelled in advance, that it could never come into being, that it was already too late'. Though she indulges in the dream for 'one last time', she has already begun the psychic journey that will end in a vision like Alma's of sterility and annihilation.

The dream visions of both Alma and Ann tend to heighten our perceptions of the real world. Like the dream vision of Old English literature, a vision in Atwood's stories is a privileged glimpse of another reality—removed in time, perhaps, or simply lurking behind the ordinary face of the real world. Many of her stories depict this irruption of the other world into the everyday—gently, as in 'Dancing Girls', or more abruptly, as in 'A Travel Piece'.

In this story Annette, a writer of travel articles whose plane goes down in the Caribbean, finds herself afloat in a lifeboat with other survivors and feels that she has penetrated beyond the screen of busy pleasure that the travel brochures offer. The 'unspoiled Eden' devoid of danger, which she herself has conspired to create, opens to reveal another and less pleasant world:

Annette looks at the sky, which is more like a flat screen than ever. Maybe this is what has happened, she thinks, they've gone through the screen to the other side; that's why the rescuers can't see them. On this side of the screen, where she thought there would be darkness, there is merely a sea like the other one, with thousands of castaways floating around in orange lifeboats, lost and waiting to be rescued.

Annette is one of several tourist figures in Atwood's fiction, including Sarah of 'The Resplendent Quetzal'. These two join a long line of outsiders in Atwood's stories—exiles, tourists, immigrants, boarders, and refugees who challenge our sense of fixed boundaries. Trapped in a world of tourist values, Sarah fights the pervasive detachment from place, an ethos that allows place to become spectacle, reducing the world (here, Mexico) to an emotionally tepid environment. Like Annette, Sarah has a personal need to get beyond the brochure, a need that has little to do with her husband Edward's desire to experience 'local colour'.

Sitting by the Mayan sacrificial well, Sarah confronts her grief for her dead child and indifference to her dying marriage. Despite her apathy, she has managed to save one precious talisman from the surrounding tourist-trap rubbish—a plaster Christ Child from a crèche, a relic of a life where miracles are possible and faith an everyday occurrence. Instinctively she hurls the plaster baby into the well, an act witnessed but not understood by her husband. This small defiant sacrifice connects Sarah, however briefly, with two religions, both offering the possibility of redeeming sacrifice, and giving her access to a plane where anguish and suffering are explicable and not in vain. Like Ann with her vision of dancing girls, and Christine who sees the scarlet ibis, Sarah has achieved a moment of visionary insight, and a glimpse into a more radiant world.

In *Bluebeard's Egg* Atwood draws a parallel between the real world and its fairy-tale equivalent, opening windows for us—not into visionary worlds, but into familiar, but newly sinister, folk-tale texts, where we recognize ourselves among the witches and elves. Atwood's stories have always displayed a consciousness of the fairy-tale patterns behind action and personality. In 'The Man From Mars', for example, the clumsy Christine measures herself against canons of beauty imbibed from such stories: 'In childhood she had identified with the false bride or the ugly sister; whenever a story had begun "Once there was a maiden as beautiful as she was good," she had known it wasn't her.' But in two stories from *Bluebeard's Egg* , the title story and 'The Sin Eater', fairy tale and folk motif are more than incidental devices; Atwood reveals them as permanent and sinister shadow texts behind the events and characters of the real world.

'Bluebeard's Egg', like 'The Resplendent Quetzal', is one of Atwood's finest stories—emotionally resonant, and breathtaking in its ability to conjure the menace that lurks in the everyday. As the third wife of an eminent doctor, a 'heart man', Sally has no intimations of menace as 'Bluebeard's Egg' opens. She professes to be complacent in her possession of Ed, who 'is so stupid he doesn't even know he's stupid'; if he belongs in a fairy tale at all, he is merely a 'child of luck, a third son who, armed with nothing but a certain feeble-minded amiability, manages to make it through the forest with all its witches and traps and pitfalls and end up with the princess, who is Sally, of course.' But the complacency of that 'of course' is partly bravado, because she is obsessed with the 'puzzle' of Ed, with his 'inner world, which she can't get at'. Sally begins to contemplate other fairy-tale models for her husband. From a night course on 'Forms of Narrative Fiction' she brings home a writing assignment on the folk-tale of Bluebeard's egg, and measures Ed against the tale's paradigms of male power and duplicity. She concludes that Ed can't be the wizard: 'he's nowhere near sinister enough.' Perhaps, then, Ed is the egg in the story, 'bland and pristine and lovely. .Stupid, too'. But this hypothesis loops back to the inner puzzle of Ed. How can a story be told 'from the egg's point of view, if the egg is so closed and unaware?' As Sally witnesses Ed's casual fondling of her best friend Marylynn, she faces the possibility that she has miscast Ed in her mental fairy story: 'Possibly Ed is not stupid. Possibly he is enormously clever.'

The strength of the story lies in its ambiguity. Ed remains an enigma; we never know if he is innocently asleep at the end of the story or pretending—'as if asleep'. Neither do we know if Sally will play out the role of Bluebeard's third wife, the one who outwits him and unmasks his villainy, or if she is destined to join the ranks of discarded wives floating dismembered in their own blood. Atwood creates a macabre echo between the fairy-tale dismemberment and contemporary heart surgery, giving Ed a mysterious, almost sexual, power over women because he sees their hearts, and even takes a knife to them.

For 'The Sin Eater' Atwood moves from the limited third-person narration of 'Bluebeard's Egg' to a first-person confessional tone, and presents another medical man, the psychiatrist Joseph, who is portrayed as a figure from folk-lore—the sin eater. In 'Bluebeard's Egg' the fairy-tale is not told until near the end of the story, but in 'The Sin Eater' the Welsh belief in the scapegoat eater of sins is prominently placed in the second paragraph. The narrator, one of Joseph's patients, sees him as the sin eater because he listens to the woes of so many unsuitable and non-paying patients; but, as in 'Bluebeard's Egg', the symmetry between tale and reality is gradually displaced. Joseph dies, and the narrator has a complicated dream in which one of his ex-wives offers a plate of cookies that a smiling Joseph describes as 'My sins'. Both stories end with visions that give the women new insight into the relation between tale and reality; this obliges them to renovate their own roles, and to identify with new and dangerous archetypes from the world of folklore. Both stories, which offer revisions of the patriarchal figure of the smiling professional man, stir up the fertile material of dream and folktale to realign our perceptions of order in the world.

'Bluebeard's Egg' is the crowning achievement of this collection; but a less flashy and disturbing kind of story also commands attention. In the opening and closing stories of *Bluebeard's Egg*—'Significant Moments in the Life of My Mother' and 'Unearthing Suite'—Atwood uses an easy 'autobiographical' style, creating the kind of personal history that is common in Alice Munro's stories, recounting believable histories into which we readily enter. These two loosely episodic stories function as book-ends to the volume, framing the other ten stories, two of which—'Hurricane Hazel' and 'Betty'—are written in a similar semi-autobiographical style.

'Significant Moments' deals consciously with the nature of family stories: their material, their audience, their function, and their power to create as well as to communicate reality. The first-person narrator finds the motivation behind some of her mother's narrations inscrutable, but comforts herself with the reflection that 'There is, however, a difference between symbolism and anecdote.' Thus the word 'significant' in the title is ambiguous, for just as the mother leaves out 'the long stretches of uneventful time' and 'cannot be duped into telling stories when she doesn't want to', so does the narrator select from her memory the stories that are 'significant' to her—not to mention the reader, who will also draw from these anecdotes a sense of what is significant.

The narrator continues to grope among the stories of her own youth and that of her mother, sorting, with little success, the truly symbolic from the merely anecdotal; she is still doing so in 'Unearthing Suite', the last story in the collection. Here the narrator begins to use stories herself as a way to 'unearth' her parents, and discovers in the process that no family story is ever merely anecdotal, that even her parents' finding of an unusual animal dropping can be a clue to the mystery that is her mother.

The exploration of story, its material and function, continues in *Murder in the Dark*, Atwood's collection of short prose pieces. The book is divided into four parts: eight meditations in an autobiographical voice; one fragmented diary-like piece of short fiction; six short essay-fictions; and thirteen prose poems—brief lyrical prose pieces, which immediately disqualify themselves from consideration as short stories. But the rest of the book maintains close contact with the genre, sometimes by commenting on the story form rather than mimicking it. *Murder in the Dark* encapsulates all the recurrent themes of Atwood's short fiction.

'Horror Comics', from Part I, evokes the familiar idea that horror lurks beneath the ordinary, as the narrator recalls the delicious scariness of licking popsicles and discussing horror comics with her friend when she was twelve, and the thrill for the two little girls when she claimed to be a vampire; but she also remembers a time when they hit a middle-aged woman with a snowball and were stunned by the hatred in her 'white-faced and glaring' look, which made horror become too real. The closing realization that 'The undead walked among us' typifies Atwood's concern throughout her stories with the veneer of life, which often glosses over spiritual death, and the manifest danger of slipping from one state to the other.

'Murder in the Dark', from Part III, takes a similar route to an unearthing of the enormities of life and art, moving from a childhood game to an adult plane of uncertainty and even anarchy. The 'game' here is both life and art; the writer emerges as a sinister murderer, obliged by the rules of the game always to lie.

But in some of the essay-fictions in Part III the tone is lighter, more satirical. 'Simmering' is a deft futurist satire on the contemporary preoccupation with male and female roles; here the question of who does the cooking shows the endless fluctuation in the boundaries of sex roles. As the men in 'Simmering' progress from backyard barbecues to complete culinary dominance, the locus of power remains unchanged: in 'the more advanced nations' the cure for women's 'kitchen envy' is widespread 'amputation of the tip of the tongue'. The visionary satirist depicts a world where 'If Nature had meant women to cook, it was said, God would have made carving knives round and with holes in them.'

The cutting humour here is maintained in 'Women's Novels' and 'Happy Endings', both of which explore conventional assumptions about fiction, exposing absurdities by taking convention to its logical extreme. Both stories are divided into precise sections, carefully designated by number or letter. Beneath this semblance of order, however, bubbles the anarchic power of words, whose duplicity and ambiguity resist containment by the numbered paragraphs. In 'Women's Novels' all sweeping generalizations bog down in the difficulties of language:

> Women do not favour heroines who are tough and hard. Instead they have to be tough and soft. This leads to linguistic difficulties. Last time we looked, monosyllables were male, still dominant but sinking fast, wrapped in the octopoid arms of labial polysyllables, whispering to them with arachnoid grace, *darling, darling.*

'Happy Endings' deals more with plot than with atmosphere and style, spoofing the possible plot combinations in the boy-meets-girl story:

> John and Mary Meet.
> What happens next?
> If you want a happy ending, try A.

But the options in A or B, or in any of the paragraphs presented, are death or dullness. There are no other endings: 'You'll have to face it, the endings are the same however you slice it. Don't be deluded by any other endings, they're all fake . . .'

It is perhaps not coincidental that Atwood's own story endings so often sidestep death or dullness by ascending to a visionary plane. While she reveals the difficulties and dangers that language presents, and the pitfalls it harbours for the reader, Atwood seems to feel most at home where language functions to reproduce interior realities, rather than the supposedly solid realities of the exterior world. By a continual challenging of language to expose its secret difficulties and powers, she has succeeded better than any contemporary short-story writer in un-sexing the English language—that is, in attaining a voice that is not the scholar's, nor the saint's, nor the siren's. Her writing has a feminist stance, but this comes more from her rethinking of the boundaries of plot, closure, diction, and voice, than from any polemic within the narrative. A bleak playfulness pervades the stories, a sense of the writer's contest not only with language and form but with the reader as well. It is the deadly seriousness of that playfulness that gives rise to much of the humour and satire, and indeed to the visionary depth, of Atwood's short stories.

6

THE BURSTING DAM OF THE SIXTIES
AND AFTER

In 1969, when Donald Stephens set out to summarize the achievements of a decade of short-story writing in his article 'The Short Story in English' (*Canadian Literature* 41, Summer 1969), he singled out 1961 as the year when 'the dam burst' with many new collections. The year following the appearance of Robert Weaver's *Canadian Short Stories* (1960) showed that writers were building on, and moving away from, the historical base represented by this seminal anthology. Never again would the Canadian short story be easily chronicled or defined. The early years of the sixties were marked by a flowering both in the sheer number of published short-story writers and in the variety of forms employed.

In this rush of new writing the modernist short story would become only one strand in a new tradition that was widening out to include American post-modernist influences and other international trends. The realistic story that was so deeply entrenched in Canadian writing was well suited to a literature that was largely regional and essentially conservative. After 1961 many writers adopted modernist narrative strategies, writing realistic stories with a limited point of view that leads the narrative through a series of pointed moments—in which psychological truths outweigh the events of plot—to the achievement of a revelation. A realistic tradition stretching back through Callaghan and Knister to D.C. Scott was extended by Norman Levine, John Metcalf, Alistair MacLeod, Margaret Laurence, and many others.

At the same time, however, there were other writers of the short story who began to experiment, trying to give it vitality by challenging its assumptions and conventions. In the hands of postmodernists and fabulators such as George Bowering, Leon Rooke, Jack Hodgins, and W.D. Valgardson, the Canadian short story took on a new look. The genesis of this divided tradition can be discerned in the story collections that appeared at the start of the sixties.

A writer who leans towards the conservative tradition in the short story is **Norman Levine** (b.1923), whose collection *One Way Ticket* (1961) would be followed by four more over the next two decades, including *Champagne Barn* in 1984. Like Mavis Gallant, Levine wrote from a self-imposed exile—he lived until 1980 in Cornwall—and his stories often deal with the pain of returning to a place outgrown. Sometimes these returns are purely imagined, but in other stories they are actual pilgrimages, as in 'By a Frozen River', in which the narrator, a writer, comes to a small town in Northern Ontario to reacquaint himself with a winter he has almost forgotten. He discovers that there is much else about himself that has been lost and must be recaptured. Like many of Levine's stories, this one has an autobiographical tone, and it skirts the facts of Levine's own life. 'A Father', a sensitive story about Jewish street peddlers in Ottawa, is inevitably coloured by Levine's own youth in that city. With regard to the distinction between fiction and autobiography, Levine says: 'Life once lived, the way you remember it is fiction.'

The form of Levine's later stories is deliberately fragmentary; connections are implicit and demand a high degree of perception and participation from the reader. 'Gifts'—about reading to the blind—is held together by patterns of image and event rather than by conflict or plot. 'Django, Karfunkelstein, & Roses' lives up to its oddly assorted title by offering discrete moments of memory—of events separated by years but stitched together by an emerging pattern of understanding on the part of the narrator. Music and roses are just two of the prominent details in this story, which is filled with sensory evocations. Levine's ability to recreate these with directness and simplicity—whether it be the smell of Jewish cooking in a small Northern Ontario kitchen, or the fragrance of roses in a Zurich villa—is fundamental to his technique. The sophisticated leanness of his work suggests a poet's respect for the depths of language. Levine maintains that the secret of his technique is that he never explains what he already knows. But such reticence in writing—genteel, subversive—is not popular, and Levine has never achieved the wide readership in Canada (his work has been widely translated in Europe) of some of the other short-story pioneers of the sixties.

Hugh Hood (b.1928) opened a prolific career with *Flying a Red Kite* in 1962. His stories unite realism and allegory, moving from a lovingly evoked world of everyday detail to a symbolic world in which all action reveals a pattern of divine action. Hood calls his fiction 'emblematic' rather than symbolic, to suggest the fusion of the concrete object with its divine essence. The kite, for instance, in 'Flying a Red Kite', is both a real child's kite soaring in the breeze over Montreal and an emblem of the human soul, raised aloft over earthly things by the holy spirit and buoyed up by divine love. Hood continued to write this unfashionably exemplary fiction in *Around the Mountain* (1967), a sequence of stories set in Montreal that are organized into a meticulous geographical, calendrical, and allegorical order. Exploiting the topography of Montreal—mountain, river, parks—he constructs a paean of praise to a diverse city and its people. The cyclical unity of the collection anticipates the structure of Hood's twelve-novel cycle *The New Age*.

Hood's stories maintain their subject matter and cyclical form into the eighties in *None Genuine Without This Signature* (1980) and *August Nights* (1985). His technique is well illustrated by the opening story from *None Genuine*, 'God Has Manifested Himself Unto Us as Canadian Tire'. In this hilarious spoof of consumer culture, Hood's young lovers, A.O. and Dreamy, live their polyester lives dreaming of the wealth of goods in the local Canadian Tire store; their literature is the *Canadian Tire Catalogue*, their only recreation shopping. They do not even care to make love any more, so cocooned are they in deodorants, foot powders, and sprays of every description. In this sanitized world good and evil have been replaced by 'amazing' and 'yecchy', and the store has become a place of worship. As in all Hood's stories, the allegorical level of significance encroaches on the reader's awareness; though the writing points to a sacred meaning, Hood never loses sight of the secular world, whose factual details he catalogues with relish. His prose, lingering over the detail of colour and shape, even over advertising jargon, caresses the consumer goods of Canadian Tire. 'Ghosts at Jarry' shows similar relish for the details of a baseball game and its players in the old Montreal stadium. This is the fiction of radicalized nostalgia; Hood harnesses our yearning for the half-remembered past to remake our vision of the future.

One of his best stories is 'The Woodcutter's Third Son' from *None Genuine*. In this dense, almost Jamesian story the middle-aged jurist John Flamborough confronts the smug complacency of his own preconceived role in life and radically alters his future. The transformation is effected by John's identification with the fairy-tale role of the favoured child of fortune, the woodcutter's third son. Like Margaret Atwood, Hood evokes our almost subconscious awareness of the fairy-tale patterns of our lives, and uses them here to subvert ordinary notions of determinism and free will. Faced with a choice of roles, fairy prince or pilgrim, Flamborough yearns spiritually for the latter, while suspecting that he is more suited to the former.

Hood was one of the founding members of a group called the Montreal Story Tellers, who got together at the end of the 1960s with the conscious aim of promoting the reading of short fiction to and by the non-literary public. Along with John Metcalf, Clark Blaise, Ray Fraser, and Ray Smith, Hood made the rounds of high schools and community groups, presenting the short story to a wide audience. Until the mid-1970s, the Montreal Story Tellers were a vital feature of the short-story scene in Eastern Canada. None of the group were Montrealers; they came from all over Canada, but they all wrote of, and out of, Montreal, and each had a distinct voice. Hood has said that he began to be influenced in his story-writing by the requirements of oral performance.

The most experimental writer in the group was **Ray Smith** (b.1941), whose story collection *Cape Breton is the Thought Control Center of Canada* (1969) is determinedly iconoclastic in form and content. In his second collection, *Lord Nelson's Tavern* (1974), Smith presents another linked series of stories, centring on a group of university friends and their meetings at a tavern. His stories display an innovative control of narrative voice. In 'Two Loves', for instance, he captures the voice of Lucy, the small-town girl whose monologue is a tissue of digressions held together by the common thread of her human warmth and frailty. Smith experiments with fragmented forms and layers of actual or possible reality in stories such as 'Break Up: From the Journals of Ti Paulo', striving to express the fluidity of boundaries in human experience and to unite form with content.

A prominent feature of Smith's stories is dark scatalogical humour and an extensive colloquial vocabulary. Along with his penchant for elaborate story titles ('Were there flowers in the hair / of the girl / who danced on his grave / in the morning?'; 'The Princess, The Boeing and the Hot Pastrami Sandwich'), this diction serves to date Smith's stories; they belong more distinctly to the sixties than do those of other Montreal Story Tellers.

At the opposite end of the spectrum from Smith's sixties' baroque lies the work of **John Metcalf** (b.1938), who came to Canada from England in 1962. He has produced three collections of pellucid, literate stories (*The Lady Who Sold Furniture*, 1970; *The Teeth of My Father*, 1975; and *Adult Entertainment*, 1986), although he has been more influential as an editor and anthologist, notably of the important series *New Canadian Stories* and *Best Canadian Stories*.

In 'The Years in Exile' (*The Teeth of My Father*), Metcalf animates a theme common in his writing—that of the writer as exile, not merely geographically but spiritually and temporally. The exile in this story is a crotchety old writer, dreaming of his childhood in England—the source, he now realizes, of inspiration for his life's work. Having exiled himself from that enchanted world of discovery in his youth in order to pursue his career in Canada, he now finds himself, towards the end of his life, exiled again—from activity, from the values of the younger generation, even from writing itself—and becomes absorbed in making a dream pilgrimage towards the bright memories of his boyhood.

Clark Blaise (b.1940), a peripatetic writer of novels and short fiction, brought his divided heritage—American, Canadian, and French-Canadian—to the colourfully assorted mosaic of the Story Tellers. Blaise's three collections—*A North American Education* (1973), *Tribal Justice* (1974), and *Resident Alien* (1986)—all display his fascination with the country of childhood, a state from which we have lost citizenship, while retaining partial rights of access. Like Metcalf, he writes from the point of view of the eternal outsider, looking at Florida, New York, Montreal, or Manitoba through the eyes of one with a dual and suspect identity who is perpetually passing through.

Many of Blaise's stories are set in the steamy landscape of central Florida, and they teem with lush images of beauty and horror. In one of his finest stories, 'Notes Beyond a History', two boys find a lost canal in the Florida swamp and enter a hidden community of mixed-blood settlers—Catholic, inbred, albino, and repulsively colourless. The terror of this discovery (almost sexual in the suggestive depiction of the fertile swamp) stays with the boys, one of whom becomes a historian, and discovers, as the story's title suggests, that some truths lie outside and beyond history. History denies the existence of a mixed-blood Catholic settlement on Lake Oshacola; memory insists on its reality. Memory here, as often in Blaise's stories, chances upon the hidden secrets of history, geography, or of the body—shameful realities that documentary evidence denies but the body affirms.

Blaise brings his talent for unearthing the hidden horror of life to a Montreal setting in 'Eyes', a *tour de force* of narration that is consistently told from a second-person point of view. The insistent 'you' in the story involves the reader in a sinister tour of a 'new country', the seedy, immigrant side of Montreal. In this city of voyeurs, the 'you' also becomes a voyeur, and is finally and perversely attracted by the repellent eyes in the head of a butchered pig in the marketplace: 'How the eye attracts you! How you would like to lift one out, press its smoothness against your tongue, then crush it in your mouth.' Blaise brings his full mastery of the prosaic diction of horror to bear on the colourful, earthy market: an amalgam of everything alien.

The sense of displacement and alienation in Blaise's stories continues in his third collection, *Resident Alien* (1986). Bracketed by two autobiographical fragments are four of his 'Porter/Carrier' stories covering the familiar Blaise territory of dual identity, here that of a family whose name changes at border crossings. As their name(s) suggest, they are doomed to 'carry' the burden of their alienation through Canada and the eastern United States.

In contrast to the work of the Montreal Story Tellers are the realistic, strongly moral stories that **Margaret Laurence** (1926-1986) began to publish around this time. Laurence's first collection, *The Tomorrow-tamer* (1963), which grew out of her residence in Somalia and Ghana, contains her strongest, most memorable stories. Thought to be outside the mainstream of Canadian literature, because of their exotic setting and subject, they have not often been anthologized—though 'The Voices of Adamo' and 'A Gourdful of Glory' were included in Robert Weaver's *Canadian Short Stories; Second Series* (1968). Laurence's second collection, *A Bird in the House* (1970), is Canadian in setting and immediately established itself at the heart of the canon both for literary study and for popular reading. Set in Laurence's fictional Manitoba town of Manawaka, these eight linked stories explore the childhood world of Vanessa MacLeod, a young artist struggling to free herself from the 'brick battlements' of an exacting grandfather and his rigidly maintained Scots heritage. Most often anthologized is 'The Loons', a lament for the passing of an entire way of life among the Indians, epitomized by the haunting call of loons. More evocative of the Canadian sensibility, however, are the stories 'To Set Our House in Order' and 'Mask of the Bear', in which young Vanessa strives to understand her grandfather's world of order and public masks, which stands in rigid opposition to her own ideals of freedom and disarray.

Also emerging from a strong Celtic background is the work of **Alistair MacLeod** (b.1936), whose stories began to appear in the pages of *Best American Short Stories* (*BASS*) in 1969. Although his first collection, *The Lost Salt Gift of Blood*, was not published until 1981, individual stories made their mark much earlier in journals and in the pages of *BASS* ('The Boat' in 1969; 'The Lost Salt

Gift of Blood' in 1975; and, on the 1972 Distinguished list of *BASS*, 'The Golden Gift of Grey' and 'The Vastness of the Dark'). MacLeod's lyrical prose captures the experience of exile from, and return to, Cape Breton society, a world of miners and fishermen bound to a piece of land or a patch of sea. MacLeod uses the seemingly commonplace dialectics of loss and recovery, giving and receiving, vision and blindness, to structure his first-person narratives, but he vividly reanimates old concepts of blood and family and belonging. His second collection, *As Birds Bring Forth the Sun* (1986), contains only seven stories, all of superior quality. Though MacLeod is not a prolific writer, his well-made stories, with their poetically exact descriptive passages and elegiac tone, represent a high level of accomplishment.

Another group of recent short-story writers—many of them female—have, like Atwood and Munro, leavened the strong Canadian tradition of realism with newer techniques drawn from the American short story. Chief among them is American-born **Audrey Thomas** (b.1935). The date of her first collection, *Ten Green Bottles* (1967), makes Thomas the first to stake out a new form and a completely new area of female experience for the Canadian short story. The lead story in this collection, 'If One Green Bottle', employs a tightly controlled stream-of-consciousness narrative to capture the experience of hospitalization and miscarriage in Africa. In later collections—*Ladies and Escorts* (1977), and *Goodbye Harold, Good Luck* (1986)—Thomas continued to use metafictional techniques to map the murky relationship between life and art, subjecting language to a fierce scrutiny that is equalled only in Atwood's stories. Etymologies, both exact and fanciful, subvert the accepted meaning of words, as in the title of one early story 'Initram' ('martini' backwards), or in a later story, 'Mothering Sunday,' which opens with this meditation on meaning:

Hail Mary, Wounded art Thou among Women. That's what it means, doesn't it? Still there in the French; *blesser*: to harm, to hurt, to injure, to wound. '*C'est une blessure grave.*' *Se blesser*, to wound oneself. In English we can trace the word back to *blōd*. Hail Mary, Blessed art Thou among women. All the Marys bleed.

Thomas also harnesses the post-modern techniques of fabulation ('The Princess and the Zucchini') and of metafiction ('The Man with Clam Eyes') to remake words and stories from a female perspective. She is not therefore purely a post-modern writer.

Although Thomas borrows techniques (disrupted temporal sequences, elements of fantasy, and obedience to fable rather than to plot) from the American post-modernists Coover, Gass, and Barth, she, like Atwood, transforms them into tools for exploring a particularly female reality whose significance and solidity are never in question.

The stories in two collections by **Marian Engel** (1933-85), *Inside the Easter Egg* (1975) and *The Tattooed Woman* (1985), are written from a similar perspective. Engel wrote short, playful stories that sometimes descend from playfulness to depths of bitterness and the grotesque, for example in 'Madame Hortensia, Equilibriste', about a retired one-legged performer who struggles to re-invent herself as an artist rather than as a freak. Some of her best are the Marshallene stories from *Inside the Easter Egg*, especially 'Marshallene on Rape', which uses a numbered sequence of statements to recreate the chatty voice of the trashy but irresistible Marshallene. With wilful female irreverence Marshallene heads one supposedly objective segment of the discussion 'Rapees I have Known'. Some of Engels' short short stories—'In The Sun,' 'Banana Flies'—have a surreal quality; here the author plays games with the boundaries between the real and the unreal, and unleashes a refreshing female view of the world.

By the 1970s the field of the Canadian short story had again widened considerably. There were many more writers whose stories—published in the pages of *The Tamarack Review, Descant, Fiddlehead, Canadian Forum, Canadian Fiction Magazine, The Malahat Review*, and *Ontario Review*—explored and made real a small portion of the world. **Jane Rule** (b.1931 in New Jersey), primarily a west-coast novelist, began to write stories of childhood worlds, and the view from there of adult rules and roles in the larger world. Well-crafted stories such as 'My Father's House', 'Brother and Sister', and 'The Bosom of the Family' epitomize her concern with the turbulent currents of family life. *Theme for Diverse In-*

struments (1975) collected also a set of stories using the powerful metaphor of the house to stand for the edifice of society's rules and expectations in which her characters live, and from which they often seek to escape: 'House', 'In the Basement of the House', 'The Furniture of Home' and 'Housekeeper'.

At about the same time, from Canada's east coast, the stories of **Beth Harvor** (b.1936) began to appear, and to gain critical approval; one of them, 'Pain Was My Portion', was published in *BASS* in 1971. This story, delicately balanced between sentiment and criticism, exposes the emptiness behind the conspicuous competence of an American couple facing the death of a close friend, and enters the contrasting world of their teenage daughter. The title is taken from a gravestone inscription found by the family in a Loyalist cemetery: 'Pain was my portion / Physic was my food / Christ was my physician / Which did me no good.' This message mirrors the story's evocation of the swings of anger and humour contained in the emotional reaction to the randomness and loneliness of death. Another of Harvor's stories, 'Our Lady of All the Distances', made the list of Distinguished Stories in *BASS* in 1972. Both stories appeared in Harvor's collection *Women and Children* (1973). Her second collection, *If Only We Could Drive Like This Forever*, was published in 1988.

In the early 1980s the influence of acclaimed writers such as Alice Munro began to be felt in the fiction of a younger group of writers. **Isabel Huggan** (b.1943) did for 'Garten', Ontario, what Munro did for Jubilee: she made palpable the atmosphere of brittle respectability and secret scandal in small-town Ontario life. Huggan traces the growth of her protagonist, Elizabeth, an intelligent overgrown girl, in a series of eight stories collected in *The Elizabeth Stories* (1984). In 'Sorrows of the Flesh' Elizabeth falls in love with a young American high-school teacher, only to discover that he beats his timid and vulnerable wife. In all Huggan's stories, dreadful knowledge lurks in the realm of secrets and the unspoken—a special territory of this writer. Like Munro, Huggan charts with deadly accuracy the protocol of family interaction and its extension into small-town life.

A male writer in the Munro tradition is **Guy Vanderhaeghe** (b.1951), whose excellent stories 'The Watcher' and 'Reunion' were mentioned in *BASS* in 1981 and 1983, respectively, and whose collection *Man Descending* (1983) won a Governor General's Award. Vanderhaeghe's technique is epitomized in 'The Watcher', where the first-person narrator, eleven-year old Charlie, undergoes a summer of unpleasant discoveries at his grandmother's farm in Saskatchewan. The often grotesque treatment of rural characters is reminiscent of Munro's early Ottawa Valley stories, although Vanderhaeghe also captures an urban world of divorced and drifting people. His typical protagonist is both unloved and unlovable, a 'man descending', caught on the wrong side of life and of women. The adolescent version of this self-pitying character is Billy Simpson, the anti-hero whose slangy, tough-talking voice belies his vulnerability in 'Drummer' and 'Cages.'

Sandra Birdsell (b. 1924) has also followed Munro into the twin territories of the small town and the human heart. *Night Travellers* (1982) is a series of stories linked by setting (the fictional Manitoban town of Agassiz) and by characters (the numerous Lafreniere family). Birdsell concentrates on the daughters, tracing the pain of artistic and sexual development in stories such as 'Truda', 'The Wednesday Circle', and 'The Wild Plum Tree'. Her second collection, *Ladies of the House* (1984), contains a more varied set of stories, although the Lafrenieres reappear, as does the stifling 'shoebox' of the small town. Birdsell skilfully creates the naïve child's perspective; in 'The Bride Doll' young Truda Lafreniere finds that she alone perceives the beauty of the grotesquely attired bride at a country wedding. Like the narrator of a Munro story, she discovers the world's hostility towards expressions of love and beauty that have not been sanctioned by society. 'Keepsake', an excellent story that gathers three women relatives around the kitchen table for an exchange of family anecdotes, ends the collection. The grandmother, Mika, realizes that time, memory, and perspective alter and deform stories and that social pressure tends to render them 'harmless and humorous, slanted'. But the reader is aware that she is withholding one story that is important to her—which, as 'Keepsake' ends, she begins to tell.

In 1984 twelve stories by **Timothy Findley** (b.1930), representing thirty years' work, were collected in *Dinner Along the Amazon*. These gentle, leisurely tales recapture another era (in 'Lemonade' and 'War'), using a confiding first-person voice to document the pain of relationships between parent and child—a hurt often felt throughout life. All of Findley's characters are the walking wounded in one sort of war or another.

Some recent Canadian short-story writers have chosen to follow the style of urban realism popularized by John Updike in the United States. **Janice Kulyk Keefer** (b.1952) and **Robyn Sarah** (b.1949) are two younger writers whose fiction covers a middle-class ground of faded dreams and compromised ideals. Sarah's highly tactile story, 'The Pond, Phase One' (included in *Best Canadian Short Stories* for 1986), is filled with the textures of the water and the mud of the pond, where two young mothers shed clothes and inhibitions in a rediscovered ecstasy of mud. Sarah blends the human situation and the natural phenomena (underground springs and surface mud) to form unsubtle, yet workable symbols. Like Kulyk Keefer in 'Mrs. Putnam at the Planetarium' (*The Paris-Napoli Express*, 1986), she makes creative use of dialogue to differentiate true conversation from social babble.

Although this fiction of qualified realism—ranging from the stories of Munro to those of the new writers in the eighties—continues to flourish vigorously with popular and critical approval, there has existed alongside it since the 1960s a brand of writing that seeks to find and break the boundaries of the short story as it was defined in the early modernist era. **George Bowering** (b.1935), a Vancouver writer of poetry and novels, is the most prominent reviser of the short story. Bowering's central contribution to the genre is, ironically, an anti-story called 'A Short Story'. This narrative is divided into sections, each headed by a term from the lexicon of the short-story critic: 'Setting', 'Character', 'Point of View', 'Protagonist', 'Symbolism'—and so on through the list of terms at the back of the high-school anthology, to 'Theme' at the story's end. Bowering explains this deconstructive impulse as the result of a 'loss of faith' in the realist story, and he continued to strike metafictional poses in *Flycatcher and Other Stories* (1974) and *Protective Footwear: Stories and Fables* (1978).

A writer who has made an important contribution to the short-story tradition in Canada is **Leon Rooke** (b.1934), an American who has adopted the Canadian West Coast as his home. He has published six collections, from *The Last One Home Sleeps in the Yellow Bed* (1968) to *The Birth Control King of the Upper Volta* (1982). His stories are remarkable for their experimental use of the single voice, often with bizarre vocabulary and unplaceable regional traits, to recount tales of psychological trauma. In stories such as 'Mama Tuddi Done Over' (*Best American Short Stories*, 1980) and 'Sixteen Year Old Susan March Confesses to the Innocent Murder of All the Devious Strangers Who Would Drive Her Down', Rooke enters fully into the persona of a character, inundating the page with a rich flow of words. Sometimes playful ('The Birth Control King of the Upper Volta'), sometimes prophetic ('A Bolt of White Cloth'), Rooke's stories also use fairy-tale motifs and structures to suggest multi-layered and ultimately elusive depths of meaning.

Rooke's prairie counterpart is **Rudy Wiebe** (b.1934), a writer better known for novels retelling prairie history. Obsessed with gaining perspective, with seeing all sides to a story, Wiebe uses his short, meditative narratives ('Where Is the Voice Coming From?', 'Along the Red Deer and the South Saskatchewan') to capture a vanished voice in history—that of the Plains Indians. Making free use of historical data and documentation, Wiebe seeks to go beyond the message of history to liberate a voice that is visionary in its origin. Much of Wiebe's short fiction speaks from outside the borders of society—for the starving Inuit woman in 'Oolulik' or for the outlaw and Mountie-killer in 'The Naming of Albert Johnson'. The latter story, a circular narrative whose form mirrors its message, is perhaps Wiebe's most anthologized piece of short fiction. His stories are collected in *Where is the Voice Coming From* (1974) and *The Angel of the Tar Sands* (1982).

A Maritime writer who concentrates on the symmetry of form and content is **Silver Donald Cameron** (b.1937), whose short stories rely for their impact on experiments with photographic effects. In 'Snapshot: The Third Drunk', and 'Composite: Double Exposure' Cameron ties the story so closely to a photograph within the narrative that the reading of it arouses the sensation of looking at a photograph. The narrative in 'Snapshot' (included in Robert Weaver's *Canadian Short Stories: Third Series*, 1978) begins with a snapshot produced in a barroom conversation, then circles away from it through a series of semi-drunken tales about the people in the photograph, and finally returns to the snapshot, the reader's eyes having been opened to what the image actually implies.

While Wiebe, Rooke, and Cameron experiment with visual and vocal effects in an attempt to alter the reader's perspective, other writers seek to marry the contemporary short story to older prose genres. In *Spit Delaney's Island* (1976) **Jack Hodgins** (b.1938) juxtaposes contemporary mythology about marital separation with ancient acts of separation—of island from mainland, of land from sea, and ultimately, of mind from self. Stories such as 'Separating', 'The Trench Dwellers', and 'Spit Delaney's Island' evoke mythical archetypes from geography and from Indian folklore to capture the essence of Vancouver Island. Hodgins acknowledges a debt to the American traditions of Southern Gothic ('Three Women of the Country') as well as to the newer Latin American movements of fabulation and magic realism. In 'At the Foot of the Hill, Birdie's School', for example, which crosses an invisible boundary between the realistic and the fantastic, the reader must forgo realism of plot. Hodgins extends this 'magic realism' to novellas as well as stories in a later collection, *The Barclay Family Theatre* (1981). In 'More than Conquerors' he explores the threshold between mortality and immortality, and raises the enticing possibility of fantastic escape from the everyday world.

The Manitoba writer **W.D. Valgardson** (b.1939) reaches back to the Gothic to find the inspiration for many stories in his three collections: *Bloodflowers* (1973), *God Is Not a Fish Inspector* (1975), and *Red Dust* (1978). In 'Bloodflowers', included in *Best American Short Stories* in 1971, a dry literary myth takes on a terrible reality for a schoolteacher on a remote island off the coast of Labrador. In this story, as in 'A Matter of Balance', Valgardson borrows from old gothic forms and from new ones (contemporary horror fiction) to achieve suspense and psychological tension. Danny Thorson cherishes a serene contempt for the superstitions of the islanders, scoffing at their belief that picking the red bloodflowers brings bad luck, saying to one of them:

> What you want is what those people had that I was reading about. They used to ward off evil by choosing a villager to be king for a year. Then so the bad luck of the old year would be done with, they killed him in the spring.

At the end of a winter in which there were many deaths, when Danny was made a leader and had been granted a beautiful girl as his mate, he panics at the discovery that the islanders are conspiring to prevent him from leaving. Valgardson employs some of the techniques of horror fiction—indirection, foreshadowing, portentous detail—in revealing gradually that Danny is living the myth of the village king.

Hodgins and Valgardson both work out contemporary myths in remote and distinctive rural societies. **Matt Cohen** (b.1942), on the other hand, conducts his fictional experiments against a solidly urban background. The title story of *The Expatriate: Collected Short Stories* (1982) evokes the ambience of Toronto's seedier neighbourhoods, where both the unemployed characters and their baseball heroes are losers. The 'expatriate' here is a scriptwriter who begins to merge with his script, discovering the expatriate within himself as he tries to construct a script about immigrant problems in Toronto. Such unsubtle psychological transitions are common in Cohen's stories, where unexpected shifts in the plane of reality replace realistic plot and dialogue as the focus of narrative interest. Some of his short pieces resemble dream sequences ('The End', 'Keeping Fit') and some ('After Dinner Butterflies', for example) blend a surrealistic world of spaceships, butterflies, and rabbits with an ordinary domestic scene. One of Cohen's best-known stories, 'Columbus and the Fat Lady', explores the obsession of a circus performer who has entered too fully into his role, reliving the conquests and trials of Christopher Columbus. The story begins with historical material, but veers into a carnivalesque world of fantasy, as we enter the mind of the performer, where the grotesque circus world (personified by the Fat Lady) merges with the high romance of Columbus's voyages.

A different urban scene is depicted in the stories of **Shirley Faessler** (b.1921), who writes about Jewish residents in Toronto's Kensington Market area. First published in the *Atlantic Monthly* and *The Tamarack Review* in the late 1960s, they were not collected until recently in *A Basket of Apples* (1988). These nine linked stories—including 'Henye', 'Intercede for Us, Auntie Chayele', 'Maybe Later It Will Come Back to My Mind', and the title story— are vivid depictions of a community the narrator grew up in and then left, and now observes with clarity and some nostalgia, but without sentimentality.

Another of Toronto's urban writers who brings a new twist to Callaghan's old territory is **Katherine Govier** (b.1948). Her stories in *Fables of Brunswick Avenue* (1985) map out a territory belonging to a middle generation, a bourgeois world of children, mortgages, and psychiatrists in which there often flashes a spark of buried passion. In a fine story, 'The Dragon', a psychiatrist is 'transported' into the world of his favourite patient, and discovers his desire to 'slay the dragon' of female sexuality and menace. The controlled, almost chronicling tone of Govier's prose mitigates her descriptions of violence and lends a precise tension to the surface of her stories.

The novelist **Helen Weinzweig** (b. 1915) is another author who experiments with the short story's potential to chart the dark regions of the human heart. In two recently anthologized stories, 'Causation' and 'What's Happened to Ravel's Bolero?', she uses a highly stylized, almost surreal patterning of events and dialogue to capture the spiralling movement of the mind under stress. Chronological time in her stories is fragmented, creating dream-like sequences of events and disrupting the balance between cause and effect, as in the paradoxically titled story 'Causation'.

Alongside these writers who play with the boundaries of the modernist short story is another group whose stories command attention less for their formal innovation than for the fresh angle on human experience they provide. Whether they speak from the ranks of the newer immigrants to Canada, or for neglected places and peoples, they give voice to parts of the Canadian experience that were once mute. **W.P. Kinsella** (b.1935), for example, has created a distinctive narrative voice for his Indian stories in *Dance Me Outside* (1977), *Born Indian* (1981), and *The Moccasin Telegraph* (1983). He has also successfully combined dreamy nostalgia and fantasy in his baseball stories, collected in *Shoeless Joe Jackson Comes to Iowa* (1908). **Paulette Jiles** (b.1943), a poet as well as a writer of stories, carves her fictional territory out of the Canadian North. In stories such as 'Night Flight to Attawapiskat' the female protagonist challenges both the seamless, hostile northern landscape and the *macho* attitudes that often make the wilderness a male preserve.

One of the earliest short-story writers to enunciate the feelings of the Canadian immigrant was **Austin Clarke** (b.1932), born in Barbados but educated at the University of Toronto. In his stories, which began to be mentioned in *BASS* in 1964, Clarke brought wry humour and a self-deprecating tone to bear on the world of West Indians new to Toronto in the sixties and seventies, achieving in stories such as 'A Wedding in Toronto' and 'Why Didn't You Use a Plunger?' a vision of exile both humorous and horrific. His stories, which are collected in *Amongst Thistles and Thorns* (1965, NCL 1984), *When He Was Free and Young and He Used to Wear Silks* (1971), and *Nine Men Who Laughed* (1986), exhibit a vital and occasionally lyrical use of dialect.

Two young writers whose stories also straddle two worlds are **Neil Bissoondath** (b.1955 in Trinidad) and **Rohinton Mistry** (b.1952 in Bombay). In his critically acclaimed collection of 1986, *Digging Up the Mountains*, Bissoondath speaks in varied voices— from that of the middle-class businessman caught in West Indian political unrest ('There Are a Lot of Ways to Die'), to that of a Japanese woman trapped by family and history ('The Cage'). Most of his characters are trapped in roles decreed by outside forces; Bissoondath ably captures the voices—defiant and pathetic—of these social prisoners in their futile struggles for dignity and autonomy.

Rohinton Mistry's *Tales from Firozsha Baag* (1987) is a series of connected short stories, all dealing with Parsi life in a cluttered and precariously bourgeois apartment building in Bombay—the

Firozsha Baag. Out of a riot of eccentric characters emerges a hero of sorts, a sensitive boy, Kersi Boyce, who exists on the periphery of the stories, until he decides to immigrate to Canada near the end of the collection. In the final story, 'Swimming Lessons', Kersi is alone in Toronto, writing a book of stories about his life in India, and taking swimming lessons, finding the chlorinated water of the local pool as foreign an element as the suburban life around him. Mistry cleverly includes within this story a commentary on and critique of his own writing. Kersi has sent his book home to be read by proud but uncomprehending parents; their discourse about its content, focus, and crucial omissions provides an interleaved, metafictional sub-text on the story and the whole collection. Mistry thus unites two traditions in the short story: the conservative, semi-autobiographical mode that specializes in connected stories of childhood; and the newer self-reflexive mode in which the function of the story is to comment on itself.

The present thriving state of the Canadian short story has been in-fluenced by both internal and external forces. The paucity of Canadian literary magazines—which for many years after the 1950s were limited to *The Tamarack Review*, *Queen's Quarterly*, and *The Canadian Forum* (though the Canadian Broadcasting Corporation's 'Anthology' and other series were additional impor-tant outlets for short fiction)—has given way to *The Malahat Review*, *Exile*, *Descant*, *Canadian Fiction Magazine*, and even *Saturday Night*, among many other magazines that publish short fiction. The use of Canadian works in school and college an-thologies has greatly increased over the last decade and a half—the clamour for 'Canadian content' has abated. Canadian writers can also be found in *The New Yorker* and *Grand Street*, and internation-al trends in fiction have made themselves felt.

I have made frequent reference in this chapter to the *Best American Short Stories* series and have taken its inclusion or men-tion of a Canadian story as a valid indicator of its excellence. Since 1915 Canadian stories in this series have been treated essentially as 'American', and have therefore enjoyed ready access to this widely known storehouse of the best in the contemporary short story. In its earlier years *BASS* set apart a section for foreign writers published in American magazines—writers such as Conrad, Mansfield, and Huxley—but in a purely token selection. Though this feature of the publication was eventually eliminated, the Canadian short story has always fared better than the 'foreign' story in *BASS*, and has benefited from the opportunity to be judged against the entire North American story output. Token representation would have hindered the recognition of new talent, but *BASS* has consistently responded to the appearance of Canadian work and to new writers. There have been periods when certain Canadian writers have appeared annually: Morley Callaghan between 1928 and 1940, and Alice Munro and Mavis Gallant in the 1980s.

In 1977 the Canadian short story was deemed to have come of age sufficiently to warrant its own 'Best' series: *77: Best Canadian Stories*, published by Oberon—one of the small presses that rapidly became the life-blood of the short story in Canada. (Inevitably, perhaps, some of the writers represented in *Best Canadian Stories* were among those represented in *BASS*: Kinsella, Valgardson, Harvor, Hodgins, Rooke, Gallant, and Munro have appeared in both.) Under the editorships of John Metcalf, Clark Blaise, Leon Rooke, David Helwig, and others, *Best Canadian Stories* has been an important national forum for the short story, even though its standards do not appear noticeably different from those of *BASS*.

Robert Weaver followed his 1960 Oxford anthology *Canadian Short Stories* with the *Second* (1968), *Third* (1978), and *Fourth* (1985) *Series*—books that collectively represent a discerning selection of Canadian work in the genre over nearly a hundred years—and in the mid-eighties he compiled with Margaret Atwood *The Oxford Book of Canadian Short Stories in English* (1986), an excellent historical anthology. Along with these and the Oberon anthologies, which have been described as 'conservative and modernist', there exist rival visions of the prescriptive shape of the Canadian short story. George Bowering's *Fiction of Contemporary Canada* (1980), for example, and Geoff Hancock's *Illusion: Fables, Fantasies and Metafiction: An Anthology* (2 vols, 1982), *Metavisions* (1984), and *Moving Off the Map: From 'Story to*

Fiction': An Anthology of Contemporary Short Fiction (1986) are anthologies that focus on a different selection of writers and narrative models. Hancock, Bowering, and other editors value a fiction of broken rules and boundaries—its essence is best captured in such terms as 'anti-fiction', 'sur-fiction', 'trans-fiction'—that, unlike the modernist offerings of the more conservative anthologies, has links to myth, dream, magic, and to the older traditions of oral fiction.

It is surely a sign of its vigour that at the end of the 1980s the Canadian short story is not in a unified state. Beyond the two main directions—modernist and post-modernist—it is pulled this way and that by the diversity of its origins. Anthologists reflect this diversity by collecting stories by region: *Stories from Western Canada* (1972), *Stories from Atlantic Canada* (1973), *Stories from Pacific and Arctic Canada* (1974), *West of Fiction* (1983), and *Toronto Short Stories* (1977) are just a few titles of regional collections. Several anthologies have been dedicated to the work of female short-story writers, for example *Getting Here* (1977), *Baker's Dozen* (1984), and the substantial collection *Stories by Canadian Women* (1984), with its companion volume *More Stories by Canadian Women* (1987).

The vitality of the genre is bolstered at the grass-roots level by several annual competitions run by local newspapers, the CBC, and various academic institutions. And contributing to the short story's popularity among readers are the many anthologies aimed at a high-school or college audience: *The Narrative Voice* (1972) edited by John Metcalf, *Personal Fictions* (1977) edited by Michael Ondaatje, *Making It New* (1982) edited by Metcalf, and *Canadian Short Fiction: From Myth to Modern* (1986) edited by W.H. New are just four collections that group stories by selected writers into teachable units, instead of trying to represent the wide contemporary diversity of the genre.

The present condition of the Canadian short story is one of forward movement. Meanwhile the recognized masters of the genre—Mavis Gallant, Alice Munro, and Margaret Atwood—chart their individual steady courses through the waves of internal dialectic between modernist and post-modernist influences. Gallant, for example, is highly appreciated both by the popular Canadian audience and by international arbiters of short-story excellence, despite the relative conservatism of her essentially modernist techniques of irony, indirection, and limited point of view. Munro and Atwood, on the other hand, offer a blend of old and new techniques that combines the sophistication of self-consciously textual fiction and the comforts of realistic issues (if not always realistic events). This borderline condition recalls the dual focus of the tales of D.C. Scott, whose *In the Village of Viger* opened the way to the modern Canadian short story by looking back to older traditions of folk tale and sketch, as well as forward to the well-made realistic story of the early twentieth century. The very flexibility of the genre, as it underwent the metamorphosis from tale to story, proved its strength. A similar strength—arising from quality, diversity, and ubiquity—should maintain its value and appeal in any new metamorphosis effected by a post-modern return from story to tale.

INDEX

(AUTHORS, TITLES)